Praise for *The Promise of Whiteness: Its Past and Its Future*

"Dr. Martha R. Bireda has completed another phenomenal treatise on white supremacy in America. *The Promise of Whiteness: Its Past and Its Future* addresses the core of white guilt in light of the recent debate about Critical Race Theory and the January 6th insurrection. American society has forced an existential deviation of Blacks and other nonwhite persons and must eradicate the difference, incomprehension, and disharmony we find ourselves in. The outrage associated with the color problem and whiteness has survived far too long. America must grasp that the presence of people of color denotes an insurance policy on humanness. Dr. Bireda challenges us to comprehend the unhealthy manifestations of the Promise of whiteness and come face to face with a throng of white supremacist tendencies. Every American must contribute to the victory of the dignity of the human spirit and act accordingly to say no to a society that continues to subjugate persons based on the false promise of whiteness. It's time to draw up the balance sheet of racial reconciliation in America."

—**Robert L. Dillingham, Jr.**, founder of the Marcus Garvey Cultural Center and former chairperson of the Black Studies Department, University of Northern Colorado; former editor, The African Holocaust Series, *Palm Beach Gazette*

"Why do many white Americans still gain psychological validation and comfort from politicians who tell them they are the 'true' Americans? How does this connect to the history of whiteness that began with slavery? Martha R. Bireda addresses these questions by breaking down 'the promise of whiteness' that was given to white laborers into four elements: place, privilege, power, and protection. Bireda thus gives us analytical tools for examining how a dichotomy was established between ruling whites and subordinate blacks that disguised class distinctions and enabled the white owners of capital to inflict alienation on white workers in the knowledge that those white workers would take out their frustration on fellow black workers rather than the ruling whites who were actually causing their exploitation and misery. This book is essential for readers who wish to connect the psychology of whiteness to the power structures of white supremacy and track that connection through four centuries of racial oppression, from slavery to the present day, using tools that will enable them to see the underlying structures of white rule."

—**Dr. Jonathan Harrison**, visiting instructor, sociology, Florida Gulf Coast University

"Martha R. Bireda again confronts the challenge of American white supremacy. Employing insights from history, psychology, and the social sciences, she powerfully describes the central challenge of American society as its 'race–based social hierarchy.' She details the tenuous white grip on the hierarchy's apex by imagining African Americans as their *essential* and *inferior* contrapose. Through the four 'P's'—place, privilege, power, and protection—whites require 'the black' for their very identity. But as Bireda explains, Barack Obama's presidential election shattered the white illusion of supremacy, exposing their historic power *and* inherent vulnerability. In her revelations, however, we can see the groundwork for the creation of a just, multi–ethnic culture that one day might realize the true American democratic promise."

—**Donald Yacovone**, associate at Harvard University's Hutchins Center for African and African American Research; author of *Teaching White Supremacy: America's Democratic Ordeal and the Forging of Our National Identity*

"In *The Promise of Whiteness: Its Past and Its Future*, Martha R. Bireda gives us a rigorous analysis of our country's current conflicts around race and class. She makes a compelling case for how much of what divides us is rooted in the misunderstanding that race exists to define our value as humans. She demonstrates that race is a construct that was developed by an elite class to divide and oppress the middle and working class of our nation. With historical research and her background as a counselor, Bireda shows the reader how the 'promise of whiteness' was used to falsely elevate the psyches of poorer whites. As that promise seemed threatened by the undoing of segregation to the presidency of a black man, many felt betrayed. Those unenlightened white folks are now comprising a backlash that ranges from micro–aggressions toward minorities to violent outbursts around the country, most notably on January 6th, 2021. Her message is from one who lived through the Jim Crow south—don't let the lie of racial supremacy and inferiority keep us from our full capacity to be loving humans."

—**Lynn Peters**, leadership and education, The Flourish Collective

"Martha R. Bireda has written a fierce and lavishly intense book that succinctly crafts Black pain and suffering within the context of Anti-Black racism while deftly examining the psyche and performance of Whiteness. By skillfully employing sociological, anthropological, historical, and rhetorical primary sources as well as effectively utilizing contemporary archival works, *The Promise of Whiteness: Its Past and Its Future* will no doubt be a pivotal and immensely valuable addition to the study of race in America."

—**Elwood Watson** PhD, professor of history, African American studies, and gender studies, East Tennessee State University; author of *Keepin' It Real: Essays on Race in Contemporary America*

"While many watched the January 6th, 2021, insurrection in shock and disbelief, Bireda shows that this event was an inevitable outcome of a deeply harmful racialized contract made over four hundred years ago. Offering a comprehensive unpacking of the historic, cultural, and psychological roots of white rage and entitlement, Bireda gives a diagnosis of the past and offers new possibilities for the future. This timely and accessible book delivers an urgent message: the 'promise of whiteness' must be denounced in order to birth a just and flourishing world."

—**Ann Gleig**, associate professor of religion and cultural studies, University of Central Florida

"*The Promise of Whiteness: Its Past and Its Future* is an important, relevant, and necessary book for our times. Martha R. Bireda has put into words what everyone needs to understand about whiteness and how to eliminate its racist and deadly effects in order to work toward making this world a better place for all people and to perpetuate equality and freedom—and possibly the survival of the world. This book should be on everyone's reading list."

—**Hy Thurman**, author, *Revolutionary Hillbilly*; co-founder, First Rainbow Coalition; co-founder and chairman, Young Patriot Organization

"I have attended many lectures, read many books, and participated in numerous gatherings regarding racism and its legacy effects. With few exceptions, I did not come away thinking that the presenters, authors, or participants did a precise job of presenting the deeply held beliefs underlying and canceling out any real progress about racism or the propping up and propagating of white privilege. Martha R. Bireda's book is clearly the exception and is the no–holds–barred message this era needs. I give the book five stars. In my opinion, the expression of 'American Exceptionalism' has such a dramatic positive appeal that it masks and hides what this country really is. Those things held up as 'exceptionalism' shine so brightly that they disguise the horror of inhumanity that created them, starting with the creation of wealth."

—**John Ashworth**, executive director, Lynching Sites Project Memphis

The Promise of Whiteness

The Promise of Whiteness

Its Past and Its Future

Martha R. Bireda

ROWMAN & LITTLEFIELD
Lanham • Boulder • New York • London

Published by Rowman & Littlefield
An imprint of The Rowman & Littlefield Publishing Group, Inc.
4501 Forbes Boulevard, Suite 200, Lanham, Maryland 20706
www.rowman.com

86-90 Paul Street, London EC2A 4NE

Copyright © 2022 by Martha R. Bireda

All rights reserved. No part of this book may be reproduced in any form or by any electronic or mechanical means, including information storage and retrieval systems, without written permission from the publisher, except by a reviewer who may quote passages in a review.

British Library Cataloguing in Publication Information Available

Library of Congress Cataloging-in-Publication Data

Names: Bireda, Martha R., author.
Title: The promise of Whiteness : its past and its future / Martha R. Bireda.
Description: Lanham : Rowman & Littlefield, [2022] | Includes bibliographical references. | Summary: "What is race-based hierarchy? The Promise of Whiteness focuses on the impact of the promise of "whiteness" upon American society in the past and future by examining its creation and evolution. Particular attention is given to the psychological needs met—and the fears, anxieties, and dissonance created by—the social construction of "whiteness""—Provided by publisher.
Identifiers: LCCN 2022015629 (print) | LCCN 2022015630 (ebook) | ISBN 9781475863550 (cloth) | ISBN 9781475863567 (paperback) | ISBN 9781475863574 (epub)
Subjects: LCSH: White people—Race identity—United States. | White people—United States—Attitudes. | United States—Race relations—Psychological aspects. | Racism—United States—Psychological aspects. | African Americans—Social conditions.
Classification: LCC E184.A1 B55255 2022 (print) | LCC E184.A1 (ebook) | DDC 305.809/073—dc23/eng/20220509
LC record available at https://lccn.loc.gov/2022015629
LC ebook record available at https://lccn.loc.gov/2022015630

To Freedom Fighters; John Brown, Viola Liuzzo, Rev. James Reeb, Andrew Goodman, Michael Schwerner, and Lillian Smith Young Patriots Organization (YPO) who embraced human completeness, rather than the promise of whiteness.

Contents

Preface		xiii
Acknowledgments		xv
Introduction		xvii
1	The Creation of the Racial Hierarchy	1
2	The Promise of Whiteness	7
3	The Psychological Power of Whiteness	19
4	Racially-Induced Dissonance	29
5	The Violation of the Promise	35
6	"It Must Not Be Again"	41
7	The Betrayal of the Promise	49
8	The Diminishing Power of Whiteness	59
9	A Changing America: Impact on the Promise	69
10	America at the Crossroads	73
Conclusion		79
Bibliography		83
About the Author		87

Preface

After spending some thirty years as a counselor and cognitive behaviorist addressing issues related to race in a variety of settings, I found my curiosity finally getting the best of me. I needed to try to fully understand how the social construction of whiteness impacts the emotional and psychological state—the very consciousness—of those designated as white. The narrative presented in several chapters in *A Time for Change* (2021), examined the psychological impact and power of the social construction of "whiteness," but questions remained. This book expands and has as its focus the emotional needs met and created by the consciousness of "whiteness."

The commemoration of the 100th anniversary of the 1921 Tulsa Massacre further served as a catalyst to examine the psychological processes which motivated racial violence and terrorism against entire African American communities. Additionally, current anxieties and fears being expressed by a segment of the white population motivates the need to answer the following questions related to the consciousness of whiteness:

- Why is the need to feel and be superior to other human beings so crucial to the identity and esteem of some whites? Does this need have

intergenerational roots? Is this need connected to intergenerational trauma?
- Why the obsessive and desperate fear of social, political, and economic equality?
- Why is black advancement and financial prosperity, in particular, so threatening?
- Why has black progress created white anger, resentment, and rage that led to the killing of blacks and the destruction of black communities?
- What are the root causes of the fear of being replaced, displaced, overruled, treated poorly by non-whites?
- Finally, as an African American, I must ask if there is something deep in the psyche of white consciousness which knows that white superiority and black inferiority are mythology?

Psychology is the study of the mind. Whiteness is a consciousness. To understand whiteness and the racism it produces, especially racial violence, it is necessary to examine the minds of those who are attached to the consciousness of whiteness. There are different degrees of attachment to this consciousness. To be clear, this book is not about "white" people but rather the consciousness of those attached to the social construction of "whiteness."

Acknowledgments

Thank you, Tom Koerner, for your consistent trust in me and the books that I propose. Thank you for your encouragement and for seeing each book to fruition. Many thanks to Kira Hall and the staff of Rowman & Littlefield for your work in the publication of this book.

Dear Colleen, I could never do this without you. You are my editor, muse, and sister. Thank you so much for your continuous encouragement and excellent editing skills.

Claire Myers, you are always so available and efficient whenever I need resources. Thank you for always being there for me.

I owe a great debt to all of those who took the time to review the manuscript and endorse the ideas contained within.

I thank members of the Flourish Collective, especially the leaders, Michele Sbrana and Lynn Peters, whose questions and comments in our study of *A Time for Change: How White Supremacy Ideology Harms All Americans*, inspired me to delve more deeply into the consciousness of whiteness.

Three authors in particular were significant in my understanding of the consciousness of whiteness: John Dollard's *Caste and Race in a Southern Town* (1957) and Davis, et. al. *Deep South: A Social Anthropological Study of Caste and Class* (1941) provided insight into the requirements of the promise for both blacks and whites.

Resmaa Menakem's *My Grandmother's Hands* (2017) provided valuable insight regarding the influence of intergenerational trauma upon white consciousness.

Finally, I must thank my greatest supporters, my children, Jaha and Saba, for their continuous support as I strive to more deeply understand human behavior and the factors that influence it.

Introduction

As America watched in shock and disbelief on January 6, 2021, an insurrection took place at the United States Capitol. The angry mob crashed through police barricades, broke windows, vandalized offices, and hoisted a Confederate flag as a noose hung outside. What explicitly has been touted as a protest against "a stolen election" has much deeper psychological and historical roots in American society. The siege of the Capitol that occurred on January 6, was the accumulation of anger, resentment, fear, and anxiety that has festered for almost sixty years. The purpose of this book is to help the reader understand the cause and the evolution of this rage.

This rage was fueled by the unfulfilled and perceived betrayal of a promise made almost 400 years ago to indentured servants and yeomen. "Whiteness," a tool for social control of the masses of those bearing white skin, ensured a sense of identity with and support of the interests of the ruling aristocratic class. Discriminatory actions, laws, racial demagoguery, and violence protected the promise of whiteness until the civil rights movement of the 1950s and 1960s. Since then, the sense of betrayal has grown as blacks, designated inferiors, became billionaires and even president of the United States. The dam of rage broke on January 6, 2021, as evidenced by the attack on the hallowed symbol of the establishment itself.

Current research and books focus on "whiteness" as the norm, on white privilege, or on the discomfort with addressing the issue of whiteness and race. There has been a failure to observe and report on the "psychology of whiteness," in particular the emotional needs met and created by the social construction of whiteness. This book expands upon two chapters from *A Time for Change*: Chapter V, "The Impact of Whiteness Indoctrination" and Chapter VI, "The Promise and Limits of Whiteness."

In this book, I introduce the idea of "racially-induced dissonance"; which happens when a physical reality conflicts with the racial mythology of the inferiority of black and other non-white peoples. The most critical and frequent response to this dissonance is racial violence and terrorism. Understanding the psychological implications of whiteness is crucial to addressing racism and racial violence.

The focus of this book is the psychosocial impact of the "promise" of whiteness; the creation, of such a promise as well as the evolution and response to dramatic changes that have taken place in American society.

CHAPTER 1: THE CREATION OF THE RACIAL HIERARCHY

During the late 1600s, the class-based social hierarchy transported from Britain was replaced by a collateral race-based hierarchy. In this chapter, the reasons why a new social hierarchy was needed and the mechanism by which it was created are examined. The essential tenet of the new hierarchy was "inequality"; no black or other non-white would ever be the social equal of any white in American society.

CHAPTER 2: THE PROMISE OF WHITENESS

The "promise of whiteness" was composed of four elements: place, privilege, power, and protection. In this chapter, each of the four elements is examined. The promised "place" was an artificially determined social hierarchy based on the mythology of white superiority; the promise included privilege and advantages that only whiteness provided or permitted. The most seductive and influential aspect of the promise of whiteness was the personal power which could be used at any time to keep non-whites, especially blacks, in subservient positions. The power also provided protection of whiteness by providing the right of whites to punish or prevent any attempts by blacks to pursue or demonstrate any form of equality.

CHAPTER 3: THE PSYCHOLOGICAL POWER OF WHITENESS

The most powerful aspect of the social construction of whiteness is the capacity for meeting the emotional needs of identity, belonging, and self-esteem of those designated as white. The identity of whiteness consists not only of the promises but also creates a set of racially-induced emotional needs, fears, and anxieties if the promise is not fulfilled or is threatened in any way. In this chapter racially-induced emotional needs, defense mechanisms, and fears will be examined.

CHAPTER 4: RACIALLY-INDUCED DISSONANCE

An artificially constructed place in society can engender a particular type of cognitive dissonance. In this chapter, the concept of racially-induced dissonance is examined. It is this particular dissonance and the emotional reaction it produces that is the catalyst for racially-motivated violence.

CHAPTER 5: THE VIOLATION OF THE PROMISE

The promise of whiteness established racial inequality as the natural order in American society in the pre–civil rights era of Jim Crow.

"Equality" is the demon that could not be tolerated by the tenets of whiteness or white supremacy. Any demonstration of blacks not staying in their "place" through their physical actions, demeanor, or any attempt to secure equal rights was a violation of the promise of whiteness; it was met with severe consequences. In this chapter, research from Hirsh (2002), Williams & Williams (1972), Wells-Barnett (1920), Whitaker (2008), and Ortiz (2006) related to perceived violations of place and the severe punishment for those violations in Elaine, Arkansas, 1919, and Ocoee, Florida, 1920, are described.

CHAPTER 6: "IT MUST NOT BE AGAIN"

An even greater violation relating to the promise of whiteness was the refutation of the mythology of white supremacy when blacks demonstrated material or economic progress in any form. The community of Greenwood in Tulsa, Oklahoma exceeded the mythology of white superiority and black inferiority. The punishment for violation of this privilege of prosperity was monumental as described in this chapter that explores the psychosocial imperative that served as the catalyst for the 1921 destruction of the "black" section of Tulsa, Oklahoma, and its inhabitants.

CHAPTER 7: THE BETRAYAL OF THE PROMISE

Wilmington, North Carolina, in 1898, dealt with the violation of the promise of whiteness and the tenets of white supremacy in the most violent way possible. The threat to the promises of whiteness relating to place, privilege, power, and protection were so grave that members of the Fusionist government (black and white Republicans, Populists) of the city were forced to leave or be killed. The way in which each of the promises of whiteness was violated is examined in this chapter. Many books describe the event itself, and this chapter will focus on the motivation for the event based on the promises of whiteness.

CHAPTER 8: THE DIMINISHING POWER OF WHITENESS

The laws and policies of the Federal Government that made blacks equal citizens, at least on paper, and a changing economy that has moved white jobs in manufacturing abroad resulted in the promise of whiteness becoming less potent. In this chapter, the ways in which working-class whites in particular have experienced and reacted to these changes is explored.

CHAPTER 9: A CHANGING AMERICA: IMPACT ON THE PROMISE

The changing demographics of the nation pose an even greater threat to the promise of whiteness. As the "browning of America" occurs through immigration, fears among a segment of whites abound. "I want my country back" is a cry for the fulfillment of the promise of whiteness. This chapter examines the impact of the nation's demographic changes.

CHAPTER 10: AMERICA AT THE CROSSROADS

The insurrection of January 6, 2021, when correlated with the Wilmington coup of 1898, was a protest against the white power establishment abandoning the promise of whiteness. The betrayal of the promise of whiteness has led to a fervor to retrieve the "place" of privileges, power, and protection that whiteness promised. In the history of our nation, violence has been the mechanism to ensure that whites not of the ruling class maintained their place at the apex of the racial hierarchy. In this final chapter, white Americans are asked to choose a new path, one that embraces a promise of equality for all citizens in what, in the twenty-first century, has become a multiracial society.

CONCLUSION: HEALING THE WOUNDS OF MYTHOLOGY

The path out of the mythology of whiteness—white superiority—is not an easy one. Disappointment and sense of betrayal prevail. Fear, anxiety, depression, and even rage are the responses. What is most definite is that the culturally-conditioned racial hatred and the mythology of white superiority will not resolve the issues posed by the failure of whiteness in the twenty-first century.

The focus of these exercises is to bring one to establish a transformative identity and to get one's emotional needs met through the practice of human completeness. Human completeness is the embracing and experience of empathy, compassion, individual awareness, and a sense of inner power. One no longer needs a phobic other to meet one's emotional needs. Only embracing personal human completeness will fill the vacuum left after releasing the mythical identity of white superiority based on generations of cultural conditioning.

Chapter 1

The Creation of the Racial Hierarchy

The colony of Virginia was established by aristocratic elites who replicated their class-based beliefs and attitudes of the Old World in the new colony, creating a class-based society completely familiar to them. At the time of the founding of the colony of Virginia, England was experiencing grave social instability evidenced by poverty, homelessness, and lawlessness. The colonies came to be viewed by England as "dumping grounds" for the "surplus" and "useless" people—the poor, homeless children, convicts, and women of questionable backgrounds. These laborers fulfilled a need in the new colonies and became virtual slaves.

Problems arose when the indentured European servants significantly began to outnumber both elite Europeans and enslaved Africans. The servants who were bound for a term of indenture believed that as a result of their labor they would obtain their freedom and opportunity for land ownership and financial prosperity. This was not to be for all who completed their service. These laborers were highly exploited, brutally treated, and not provided the opportunities of which they hoped. This cruel and hostile treatment of European indentured servants started to diminish the supply of Europeans willing to work in the colonies. The colonies looked increasingly to the enslavement of Africans.

As a result of their discontent, during the late 1660s, the indentured servants rose in a series of rebellions, the most spectacular being Bacon's Rebellion. The class-based social hierarchy of the British aristocracy was violently attacked by a multiracial group of indentured, enslaved, and yeomen Europeans, Africans, and Native Americans.

The aristocratic elite responded to the threat of rebellion, especially one of multiracial composition, by creating a new social hierarchy based upon skin color—"whiteness." According to Roediger (2007), the concept of personal whiteness rose from the realities of class division and class rule. A race-based binary system clarified by skin color—white or non-white "other"—was created, with those perceived or designated as "white" placed at the summit of the hierarchy.

Whites were perceived and treated as humans, while blacks and other non-whites were to be considered subhuman. The hierarchy designated the "other" as undeserving of freedom, social, political, economic, and human rights. The superior "place" of whites on the hierarchy provided special advantages, privileges, power, protection, and unequal distribution of the like based upon skin color.

"Whiteness," placed at the apex of this race-based social hierarchy, enabled indentured and common Europeans to gain a social status unavailable to them in their home countries. The "whiteness" they gained only marginally changed their material and economic conditions, but it was a powerful psychological mechanism for creating a sense of status, dignity, and esteem they had previously never experienced nor dreamed they could.

The collateral racial hierarchy elevated those at the bottom of the rigid class system as peasants in Britain and yeomen in the colonies to a higher place/position on the new "racial" hierarchy. Ultimately, the racial hierarchy offered a reprieve from the rigid class hierarchy which included brutality and oppression that had existed for generations in Europe. The racial hierarchy lifted the newly "white" and their descendants from the former "inferior" status to which they had been relegated. These "white" individuals could now affirm that regardless of their condition, "I am better than a black."

"Whiteness" was the ingeniously created social construct of a ruling class to preserve, maintain, and perpetuate the wealth and power of themselves as the colonial elite class-based society; and as a means to maintain control over common whites and enslaved blacks. In reality, the new social status was an illegitimate superiority, a made-up category with no biological or scientific foundation. It was an identity creating a myth of white superiority to maintain their own hegemony. There is no scientific or biological evidence that whiteness is superior to others in any way physically, culturally, or morally.

This powerful psychological tool served several critically important needs for the powerful elite by:

- Creating "whiteness" as the norm for being human; the "other" as subhuman.
- Creating an "other," a pariah group on which to focus anger and contempt rather than on the elite.
- Creating an "other" to which they assigned negative stereotypical images that provoked emotions of anger, contempt, disgust, and most importantly fear.
- Creating skin color as a value to be possessed.
- Providing a sense of personal psychological and material power based upon the tenet of white superiority.
- Promising an infinite power to be superior to non-whites.
- Creating the emotional need and motivation to focus on the other, in this case the black in particular, to keep him in his place by any means.
- Creating a "racially based" cognition and emotional response that prevented the development of "class consciousness" among common whites.
- Eliminating the possibility of a multiracial alliance or rebellion based upon common life conditions.
- Establishing "whiteness" as superordinate in power and prestige.
- Providing a way to control black bodies and white minds.

THE MYTHOLOGY

The newly created racial hierarchy was undergirded by the myth of white superiority versus black inferiority. Whiteness is based upon the ideology of white supremacy. Its tenets hold that white skin is superior to black skin, in particular, and other non-white skin. While there is no biological or scientific evidence to support the theory of white skin producing a superior human in character, cognition, culture, or morality, it is a powerful lie to incentivize and to identify with the skin color of the elite, to feel a sense of belonging and connection to the interests of the ruling class despite a gaping difference in social class.

The mythology of white superiority is reinforced and perpetuated through a set of erroneous beliefs about the inferiority of blackness that evolve over time as needed in response to any new threat of racial equality. The mythology of white superiority expresses and justifies the ideology of white supremacy. The tenets of white superiority and black inferiority create a belief system based upon false assumptions, misperceptions, omissions, and distortions, or, in other words, outright lies that upheld or undergirded a racial hierarchy. This belief in white superiority and black inferiority is buried deep in the collective subconscious of white Americans.

As was described in *A Time for Change: How White Supremacy Ideology Harms All Americans* (2021), white superiority can be and is only expressed in comparison and opposition to blackness. Without the counterbalance of black inferiority, white superiority is an empty social construction. Black inferiority is the complementary ideology of white superiority. Whiteness is defined by what it is not—the negative stereotypical images of blackness. Stereotyping of blacks has been the key mechanism for reinforcing and perpetuating the myth of white superiority. Bireda (2021) describes three major black inferiority myths: intellectual, cultural, and moral; these are used to justify the enslavement and oppression of blacks.

According to Mills (1994), "Whiteness is defined in part in respect to an oppositional darkness, so that white self-conception of identity, personhood, and self-respect are then intimately tied up with the repudiation of the Black Other." No matter how poor one was, one was still able to affirm the whiteness that distinguished one from the subpersons on the other side of the color line. The core belief of white supremacy ideology is that blacks are innately inferior to whites intellectually, morally, and culturally. It is believed that because of "black inferiority," it is normal, natural, and permissible to dehumanize blacks and to have unequal distribution of rights, resources, opportunities, and even protection under the law. This belief system that was inculcated into a promise of whiteness overshadowed class inequalities and the power of the oligarchy that without this insidious persuasion would have been otherwise obvious to the lower-class whites.

THE EXPECTATIONS OF "WHITENESS"

Those perceived and designated as "white" must adhere to the "racial contract" to surrender to the white world, conform to the social construction of whiteness rules by maintaining and sustaining the mythology of white superiority in thought, word, and actions (Mills, 1997). It is also expected that these individuals protect personal and group whiteness from threats of non-whites to equal rights and opportunities.

CONCLUSION

Whiteness is based solely on a mythology created by the ruling class for the purpose of controlling the common white population to cover the backs of the white oligarchy. Who are white changes depending on the social and economic conditions of those previously considered non-white to affirm the beliefs and rules of whiteness. The social construction defines place/position on the racially based social hierarchy, and it provides individual and group privilege and power to those perceived and designated as white. The construction invented cultural practices, values, norms, and actions designed to consistently create, maintain, and perpetuate white domination and power.

"Whiteness" provides the default standard by which non-whites are compared. It is a system of privilege associated with white identity. "Whiteness" became the norm for American society early on; America is still perceived to be a "white" country. "Whiteness" is fluid; however, the definition of who is considered to be "white" can be changed and enlarged over time. To maintain power, laws have been conscripted to this day, and churches and institutional customs fell in line to enforce a racial hierarchy depending ultimately on force.

Chapter 2

The Promise of Whiteness

The promise of whiteness is central to American societal structure. Whiteness provides the foundation for racial oppression through institutional economic, political, and social discrimination. The promise as designed rationalized the white "place" in the racial hierarchy, insured white privilege, and granted protective power to reinforce white dominance through racial terrorism and violence. The promise also creates "racialized" needs, emotions, fears, anxieties, and reactions activated when white "place" in the social hierarchy is threatened or perceived to be threatened in any manner.

THE PROMISE: PLACE

The "promise of whiteness" established a collateral racial hierarchy. The promised "place" was an artificially determined social hierarchy based upon the mythology of white superiority. The social construction of "whiteness" promised those with white skin a superior "place" in the American social hierarchy; a position in which they would have no equals. Whiteness establishes a consciousness or awareness of who one is, one's identity, one's value, and one's position in the world—an infinite superiority untouched by non-whites.

Whiteness promised the essential gift of freedom in two aspects to those who possessed it. First, whiteness promised the hallmarks of American democracy—freedom of speech, movement, decision, and opportunity to pursue the American Dream of life, liberty, and the pursuit of happiness. Second, an essential aspect of the promise of whiteness is its assurance of "inequality" in terms of freedom, rights, and opportunities to those who are not white; in this case, especially blacks.

The lack of equality for non-whites is the primary tenet of the construction of whiteness. The lack of equality is the measure of one's place in the hierarchy. The promise of whiteness consisting of four "P's": place, privilege, power, and protection ensured that social, political, and economic equality for non-whites would never occur.

The supreme promise of whiteness was social inequality for non-whites, particularly blacks. The Emancipation provided freedom from enslavement, and Reconstruction, the brief period from 1865 to 1877, offered blacks a glimpse of what social equality could feel like. This experiment in social equality, the ultimate betrayal of the promise of whiteness, was not to last. Political manipulation and principally violence were utilized to put blacks "back in their place." Black codes—encompassing the conduct of blacks and Jim Crow laws, which were state and local statutes that legalized racial segregation—and customs secured white supremacy again. The emotional need to feel superior to and to dominate blacks was restored.

The cardinal sin in relation to the racial hierarchy is "equality" for blacks and other non-whites. Social equality in terms of race is considered a menace, a threat to white dominance, and as such, any ideas, attitudes, or actions which promote equality in any form must be diminished. "Whiteness" has no value if the other is perceived or granted equality in any sphere. Equality is the core *violation* of white supremacy.

The "place" of whites and blacks in American society has been established since the creation of the social construction and reinforced with the enslavement of Africans: on March 21, 1861, the vice president of the Confederacy, Alexander H. Stephens, defended slavery saying, "Its foundations are laid, its cornerstone rests upon the great truth, that the negro is not equal to the white man; that slavery . . . subordination to the superior recoils his natural condition." The infamous *Dred Scott v. Sanford* case further perpetuated the "place" of blacks in the American racial hierarchy when Chief Justice Roger Taney stated that "as an inferior, they [the negro] had no rights which the white man was bound to respect; and that the negro might justly and lawfully be reduced to slavery for his benefit."

According to the Mudsill theory, "there must be as there has always been a lower or underclass for the upper classes and the rest of society to rest upon." This was articulated by James Hammond, a plantation owner and United States Senator from South Carolina. Hammond, who argued that "every society must find a class of people to do menial labor, whether called slaves or not, and that assigning that status on a racial basis followed natural law."

The Core Expectations of White Place

- As a white, I am superior to all other races.
- Non-whites are inferior and have no right to any social, political, or economic equality with a white.
- As a white, I must conform to the racial contract by conforming to the rules of whiteness.
- No black shall be allowed to enjoy equality of democratic rights.
- Equality for blacks and non-whites diminishes my safety, security, and power.
- As a white, I must defend and protect my whiteness at all times.

THE PROMISE: PRIVILEGE

The privilege provided by the promise of whiteness was designed to ensure white dominion in all societal and cultural institutions. Whites were to have advantages in accessing opportunities in education, politics, health care, housing, law enforcement, and the economy. The promise of privilege ensured that the safety and security needs of whites would be met. Privilege provides unequal access to emotional security, financial security in employment, social welfare, property, law and order, and freedom from fear.

The stereotypes of the ignorant black, criminal black, lazy and irresponsible black only suited for menial labor—and even the belief that black bodies did not feel pain in the same ways as whites—were used to provide whites advantages in all areas of society.

The right to vote was the major privilege that would make blacks the social equals of whites. It was the denial to blacks of the right to vote that engendered great hostility, resulting in racial terrorism, as we will see in chapter 5. Blacks were not hired for "white only" jobs and were paid less than whites for the work they did. Black schools were underfunded, and health care for blacks was segregated and limited.

A crucial aspect of the promise of privilege was that blacks could not exceed whites in the acquisition of land, material goods, or wealth in any form. The prosperity of blacks was a key element fomenting individual and collective resentment and violence toward blacks.

> The advantages white people had accumulated were free and usually invisible and so conferred an elevated status that seemed natural and almost innate. White society had repeatedly denied people of color economic benefits on the premise that they were inferior; those unequal benefits then reified the hierarchy, making whites economically superior. (McGee, 2021)

The Core Expectations of White Privilege

The promise included advantages that only whiteness provided or permitted:

- There would be no equal political, social, or economic access and opportunity.

- *All* privileges are unequally distributed between whites and blacks.
- Whites receive the greater portion of all economic and social rewards.
- White privilege creates a division of labor based upon skin color; the unpleasant, menial, and poorly paid jobs are relegated to blacks.
- Whites will hold superior positions over blacks; as a white will never be reduced to working under an inferior black.
- Blacks will be assigned to inferior jobs, whites to superior jobs.
- Whites have access to highly paid jobs.
- No black man shall have more material and economic prosperity than any white men.
- Whites would have all control over prestige and privileges.

THE PROMISE: POWER

The most seductive and influential aspect of the promise of whiteness was the personal power which could be used at any time by any white to keep non-whites, especially blacks, in subservient positions. This power granted complete control over the "other": dominion over voice, mannerisms, demeanor, lack of assertion or anger, when around whites. The promise ordained the power to define and demean blacks with negative stereotypes. This promise of personal and collective power *over any black* was most evident during the Jim Crow era.

The Core Expectations of White Power

- I hold all personal and collective power.
- I can impose my will upon the non-white in terms of my decisions and actions.
- I have the power to punish blacks for any mannerisms or actions that do not demonstrate his or her sense of inferiority and respect for my superiority.

Chapter 2

THE PROMISE: PROTECTION

The promise of protection provided whites the knowledge and expectation that the law—police and the courts—would represent and be responsive only to their interests. In addition, most crucially, the society, public opinion, and the legal system sanctioned all efforts on the behalf of whites individually and collectively to prevent and punish any perceptions or attempts by blacks to achieve social, political, or economic equality. This power that whites possessed was especially prominent during the Jim Crow era, as laws and public opinion protected those who committed racial terrorism against black individuals and communities.

Crimes committed against blacks were not considered as crimes but merely punishment for black malfeasance. Juries and courts were not expected to convict white men of violence toward blacks. Take for instance the murders of the black youth Emmitt Till, fourteen years of age, and thirty-seven-year-old civil rights activist Medgar Evers. White men, Roy Bryant and J. W. Milan, abducted, tortured, and murdered the youth. Till's decomposed body was found on August 31, 1955, three days later. An all-male and all-white jury acquitted the two *white men* of murder after deliberating for less than an hour.

Medgar Evers was gunned down in his driveway in Jackson, Mississippi, on June 12, 1963. Two all-male and all-white juries deadlocked and refused to convict Myron Beckwith. Thirty years later, conviction was achieved through the efforts of Myrlie Evers, wife of Medgar, when Beckwith received a life sentence some thirty years later in 1989.

The two case studies of racial terrorism against black communities detailed in chapters 5 and 6 will provide additional evidence of the protection provided by the promise of whiteness.

The Core Expectations of the Protection of Whiteness

- No white shall ever be punished for "correcting" a black.
- Blacks are deserving of any violence directed toward them.

- There are no rights that I as a white man have to respect in regard to blacks.
- I am legally protected from conviction from any so-called crime against a black.

THE JIM CROW ERA

The Jim Crow era provided the greatest opportunity to experience "whiteness" in America. The construction of laws, rules, regulations, customs, and etiquette created social relations that satisfied the promise of place, privilege, power, protection, and the psychological needs of identity, belonging, and esteem. Racial rules ordered life routines and social interactions, ensuring social distance and separation. Jim Crow laws and customs required a visual demonstration of black inferiority. This demonstration of black inferiority reinforced the psychological sense of white superiority, esteem, and identification with the white elites.

Davis (1941) describes a set of beliefs or sanctions for the subordination of the Negro during the Jim Crow era:

- Blacks were believed to be inherently inferior; immutably and everlasting.
- Blacks were subhuman; mentally inferior, biologically primitive, and emotionally underdeveloped.
- Blacks are insensitive to pain, incapable of learning, and animal-like in behavior.
- Blacks are unclean; the color of black skin is abhorrent, and contact with them may be contaminating.
- It is the "will of God" that blacks be sanctioned for subordination.
- Blacks are unsocialized and lack social restraints approved by whites.
- Blacks are lazy and will not work except under compulsion of force.
- Blacks are irresponsible and do not anticipate and prepare for future needs.

- Blacks are dependent upon white people and prefer this dependency to the struggle of existing in the present society without this protection.
- Blacks lack respect for property and will steal with no feeling of guilt and will lie whenever it suits them.
- Blacks lack emotional stability: quick to laugh or cry; will maim or kill without regard to possible consequences.
- Blacks lack white man's concept of sexual morality; they are sexually promiscuous.
- Blacks are childlike and will never grow up, never be completely socialized.
- The black's irresponsibility imposes a sense of certain responsibility for him from whites.

Expected Demonstration of Black Inferiority: Accommodation

Jim Crow laws and customs were used to symbolize the separate and subordinate status of blacks. In no way was there to be any indication of social equality between whites and blacks. The behavior of both blacks and whites must indicate that they are socially distant. Whites as well as blacks are subject to the laws and customs of Jim Crow. Both blacks and whites would be punished for the violation of this principle. If whites disobeyed the rules of conduct, they would encounter disapproval from other whites and could become outcasts or even harmed as those were during the civil rights movement. Blacks must exemplify in disposition and behavior that whites are superior in power and prestige.

- Blacks were to exhibit deferential behavior in the presence of whites.
- Blacks were to use a title when addressing a white.
- Whites must never use titles of respect when addressing blacks, use first names only.
- Blacks should stand back and wait until whites are served in a place of business.

- Blacks should give way to whites on streets and sidewalks.
- Blacks should go to back doors of white homes.
- Under no circumstances may a black contradict a white or insinuate that a white is lying.
- Under no circumstances may a black curse a white or express any anger or antagonism.
- Blacks must demonstrate humility in offering opinions to whites.
- Most crucially, blacks must demonstrate that they not only observe the rules of deferential speech and behavior but accept them as proper and right. They must accept their place on the racial hierarchy willingly and cheerfully.
- In all ways, blacks must show that they respect the superiority of whites. They must be humble, have the proper attitudes toward whites, and know their "place."

According to Davis (1941), "This body of beliefs constitutes an ideological system which is used to justify social relationships between superordinate whites and subordinate Negroes." Dollard's (1957) studies of race and class in the South suggests that the black accommodation to code of black-white relationships involved for the black the renunciation of protest or aggression against the conditions of his life. Dollard suggest that it is important to understand the psychological process that mass accommodation involves, especially, the psychological needs of whites met by the accommodation of blacks during the Jim Crow era.

Lynching

During Jim Crow, blacks were murdered, driven from their homes, and their communities were destroyed. Lynching, however, was the weapon most often used to punish—and also to frighten—blacks into compliance with the rules and practices of white supremacy. The Equal Justice Initiative (2015) reported that 4,000 blacks were lynched during the Jim Crow era.

Cox (1945) provides the most comprehensive examination of lynching, its purpose and protection. He states that "lynching is a symbolic act of homicidal aggression committed by one people against another through mob action for the purpose of suppressing some tendency in the latter to rise from an accommodated position of subordination or for subjugating them further to some lower social status." Cox describes what he refers to as a recognizable lynching cycle as follows:

- A growing belief among whites that Negroes are getting out of hand in terms of wealth, racial independence, and in attitudes of self-assertion, especially as workers.
- Continual critical discussion about Negroes among whites resulting in an attitude of racial antagonism and tension.
- The rumored or actual occurrence of some outrage committed by a Negro upon some white person or persons. The ideal act is the rape of a white girl.
- The mob takes action, lynches the Negro, and blacks are terrified and intimidated; within two or three days the mob achieves its "emotional catharsis" and there is new "interracial adjustment."

It is extremely important to consider according to Cox that lynching in the South was not a crime, thus the perpetrators are fully protected by the promise and the sanctioning of the action by the white community. Cox describes lynching as "being crucial to the continuance of the racial system in the South and a powerful and convincing form of racial repression operating in the interest of the status quo."

Although the power of whiteness is primarily psychological, during the Jim Crow era, whites were the beneficiaries of material and economic advantage. Jim Crow laws mandated social segregation and discrimination. However, the unequal treatment of blacks was evidenced at the federal level as well. The advantages given to whites with regard to the New Deal and the GI bill are examples: "Between the era of the New Deal and the Civil Rights Movement, these and more government policies worked to ensure a large, secure, and white middle class" (McGhee, 2021).

While the New Deal transformed the lives of workers with minimum wages and overtime laws the job categories in which blacks were employed, like domestic and agricultural work, were excluded. While the GI Bill of 1944 paid the college tuition of hundreds of thousands of veterans, few black veterans were able to benefit. Postwar homeownership was a benefit to three out of four white families, but with federally sanctioned housing discrimination, the black and Latina rates stayed at around two out of five despite the attempts of veterans of color to participate (McGhee, 2021).

CONCLUSION

The black place in the racial hierarchy was determined by belief in the natural inferiority of the race and the beliefs that blacks were dependent, childlike, irresponsible, and needing the direction and paternalism of whites to exist in the society. The core premise of the promise of whiteness is the denial of racial equality. White's place in the racial hierarchy requires, even demands, that racial equality of any form, be it social, political, or economic, never be achieved. Any thought, perception, or intention of racial equality is a direct violation of the promise of whiteness.

The Jim Crow era was a time of definite white superiority in terms of laws legalizing racial segregation and required racial etiquette. Is the slogan "Make America Great Again" reminiscent of this period in American history? Does a certain segment of the white population need a return to the psychological satisfaction of the Jim Crow?

While the promise of whiteness provides for the aspects of place, privilege, power, and protection, it is most powerful in meeting the psychological needs of whites, especially those most attached to the consciousness of whiteness. In addition, the needs, anxieties, and fears created by the promise will be examined as well in chapter 3. It appears that the primary threat to the white psyche is the demon of social equality that would undermine the sense of domination that is required for the white sense of self and esteem.

Chapter 3

The Psychological Power of Whiteness

The social construct of whiteness is designed ideologically to meet both the safety/security and psychological needs of those designated as white. Privilege provides unequal access and opportunities for safety and economic security. If the white sense of safety and security (financial, employment, social welfare, etc.) are threatened, these too have components that must be addressed as psychological needs.

The true power of whiteness lies in its meeting the human emotional needs of identity, belonging, and self-esteem. The new collateral hierarchy based on skin color offers social, political, and economic advantage, but its essential element provides the desired psychological effect which is a boost to the sense of identity, belonging, and esteem for those at the lowest level of the class hierarchy.

IDENTITY

As human beings, our identity need is to present ourselves to others and be thought of in a desirable way. We are deeply driven by our sense of identity, that is, who we are. "Whiteness" creates a sense of identity through skin color and intensifies the need to affirm one's individual and collective white identity of belonging to the white race. Whiteness provokes the need to be thought of as a superior being. White identity is of crucial importance in our racialized society where one drop of black blood is capable of condemning a person to the status of "other" or subhuman undeserving of freedom and equal rights.

Bracher (2009) suggests that defining another group as subhuman or inferior enables individuals to maintain their own sense of self against threats to their identity. "By identifying other groups as inferior to themselves, people can have recourse at any time to downward social comparison, the process by which one selectively measures one's own status against that of perceived inferiors in order to arrive at a more positive sense of self." He suggests further that the other as inferior tends to minimize one's own lack of status and recognition. We define ourselves by comparison and contrast with others; the white sense of identity is degraded when he or she fails to be better than a black.

Belongingness is the human emotional need to be affiliated and accepted socially. The social construction of whiteness connects those of white skin and provides according to the racial hierarchy a superior identity. This need for belongingness has historical roots originating in Europe with the rigid class system where the majority of residents were of the peasant class. Affiliation and alignment with the ruling class has been a powerful race consciousness since whiteness was created. Just as the indentured European servants embraced the consciousness, historically the sense of belonging and connection to the ruling class by way of skin color continues to have potent appeal.

According to Bireda (2021), "whiteness" is most powerful in meeting the emotional needs of whites who feel they have been degraded and oppressed by their lower social status in society. Historically, the construct of whiteness has also been a powerful antidote to feelings of envy, anger, and resentment toward the elite. White racial belonging provides an illusion of opportunity for whites of all classes to become billionaires, to become one of the elite classes. Attachment to whiteness provides whites who do not belong to the elite class a sense of belonging, self-worth, hope, and control.

Racial violence, for example, became potent in creating a sense of racial connection and belonging. Lynching was a ritual in which whites of all social classes connected. DuRochner (2011) describes lynching as a "collective sense of race-based identity which minimized class distinctions."

ESTEEM NEEDS

Esteem is a human emotional need borne out of desire for social acceptance and status. Maslow (1943) described two sets of esteem needs; one consists of people's desires for achievement, competence, and mastery; the other consists of people's desires for admiration, status, and respect from others. Positive feelings about the self are necessary for overall emotional health and well-being. Whiteness provides a sense of esteem by one's position at the top of the racial hierarchy. Class anxiety can lead to feelings of inferiority and low esteem.

The construction of whiteness encourages a sense of self-worth reliant upon external reinforcement and based on comparison of one's white superiority with the black's innate inferiority. The more attached one is to the consciousness of whiteness, the more racially based validation he or she needs especially when experiencing class-related anxiety.

Racially conditioned esteem based upon the validation of white skin over black becomes problematic when experiencing racially-induced dissonance. Racially-induced comparison with a black of a higher social or economic status can reduce white esteem and lead to a need for restoration of that white esteem. Racial insults and resorting to racial violence are mechanisms for restoring white esteem.

Self-esteem provided by whiteness was especially prevalent during the Jim Crow era. If one was experiencing a sense of low self-esteem, he or she might seek respect from a black through the demonstration of black inferiority to restore his or her sense of esteem. The deferential behavior expected of blacks in terms of mannerisms, speech, even posture confirmed white superiority and the power that went with it.

Imagine the escalation of white esteem when he or she could demand that a well-dressed black man leave the sidewalk and let him pass, get respect by the black tipping his hat, or lowering his gaze. Jim Crow laws in particular built the self-esteem of whites regardless of social class as blacks were forced to go to back doors and separate entrances and sit in the back of buses. Racial violence was also implicated in building white male esteem; it reinforced identification and connection with other whites despite social class—leaders of mobs were given acceptance, attention, and support.

RACIALLY-INDUCED EMOTIONAL NEEDS

Just as whiteness meets certain emotional needs, a construct based on a mythology will be unable to meet needs provoked by the structure itself. The construct of whiteness creates a set of racially-induced needs that induce anxieties about one's status or fears about loss of advantage that must be addressed.

Racially-induced emotional needs involve manipulating black people by demanding that they play roles to validate the distorted reality or fantasy of white superiority. This need involves forcing a distorted reality of white superiority upon blacks. This is done through racist scripts of deferential and subservient behavior demanded of blacks. If this need is not fulfilled or is violated in some way, punishment in the form of violence awaits the offender or offending community. These violations are usually related to the desire of blacks to attain social, political, or economic equality in some way.

NEEDS RELATED TO TRANSGENERATIONAL TRAUMA

The obsessive and often compulsive need to maintain a place of superiority, control, and dominance can be considered related to what two researchers regard as intergenerational trauma. According to Bracher (2009), social and cultural forces, especially intergenerational ones, have produced damage to identities. He suggests that the migratory experience of ancestors coming to America may have been preceded by persecution, wartime flight, and extreme poverty. Also, the experiences these immigrants may have suffered when discriminated against and degraded until they became "white" created psychological needs related to racial identity.

Menakem (2017) provides evidence that suggests it is possible that generational and collective trauma suffered by whites at the hands of more powerful whites makes them vulnerable to embracing the construct of whiteness and tenaciously guarding the consciousness of whiteness.

- "Many of the English who colonized America had been brutalized or had witnessed great brutality first-hand. Others were children and grandchildren of people who had experienced such savagery in England."
- "But well before the United States began, powerful white bodies colonized, oppressed, brutalized, and murdered other less powerful white ones. This carnage was perpetuated on Blacks and Native Americans as an adaptation of longstanding white-on-white practices. This brutalization created trauma that has yet to be healed among white bodies today."
- "The concept of the Negro was created to help white Americans deal with the hatred and brutality that they and their ancestors had themselves experienced for many generations at the hands of more powerful white bodies. The phantasm of race was conjured to help white people manage their fear and hatred of other white people."

As we examine the psychological appeal of whiteness, we must ask and consider how treatment of European peasants—indentured and other yeoman—impacted the sense of self, the sense of inferiority experienced by whites. The highest place on the racial hierarchy offered a reprieve from a lower inferior status for many and the designation of blacks as the lowest, most inferior group met—and still meets—a powerful psychological need.

RACIALLY-INDUCED DEFENSE MECHANISMS

Defense mechanisms are unconscious psychological responses that protect individuals from feelings of anxiety, guilt, shame, and threats to self-esteem. Projection in particular is a mechanism that the construct of whiteness provides through the "protection" aspect.

Projection is the psychological mechanism by which the white individual engaging in racial violence attributes his own unacceptable impulses and motives to black individuals. By accusing the victim of having the thoughts and feelings that they themselves are having, whites committing inhumane acts upon blacks are able to avoid responsibility for their behaviors. Stereotypes of the black male as an aggressive, savage, and violent "brute", made it easy to spread rumors that blacks were planning to rebel and engage in killing whites. This conveniently deflects blame from whites onto black victims of racial violence.

(Bracher)He suggests that "the negative qualities attributed to blacks distracts attention from the perpetrators and redirects tit, along with derogation, hatred, aggression, and violence toward what he terms the 'subaltern '(phobic objects) black group. In addition, the perpetrators act out their own repressed qualities and impulses, including laziness, ignorance, self-indulgence, and aggression in relation to the subaltern."

Displacement

Displacement is a psychological defense mechanism whereby feelings and actions can be redirected from their legitimate target to a less threatening one. Anger provoked by white class anxiety and sense of inferiority is often directed toward defenseless blacks rather than the economic system and plutocrats who control the system.

RACIALLY-INDUCED NEEDS

The socially constructed identity of whiteness consists not only of the promises but also creates a set of needs, fears, anxieties, and dissonance if the promise is not fulfilled or if it is threatened in any way. An artificially constructed "place' engenders a peculiar set of status anxieties and racially-induced fears for individuals who are firmly attached to the consciousness of whiteness.

These needs include the following:

- An obsessive concern with blacks.
- Engaging in individual and group racial comparisons: that is, progress, etc.
- Concerns about reverse racism.
- An obsessive desire to dominate and control blacks and non-whites.
- Assurance that whites will not be replaced or displaced in terms of ability to dominate and control.

RACIALLY-INDUCED FEARS

Because the satisfaction of the emotional needs produced by the construct of whiteness require the black other, who is the subhuman inferior, there is the constant fear of the black other if he is not controlled or dominated. The value and power of the whiteness that comes from an external source is dependent upon the mythology of black inferiority and comparison to blackness. The question arises, "What makes whiteness superior for its own sake?"

Eminent historian, John Dollard (1957), says that "In the end, it seems a better statement to say is that white people fear Negroes." He says there is a long-enculturated history of fear of the Negro, fear of revolt, running away, and isolated assault. Dollard suggests reasons for this fear:

- The Negro will attempt to claim any white prerogative or gain, that is, equality.
- Whites will constantly fear him [the Negro] because of his hope of personal advancement and striving; whites and Negroes are in continued actual or potential opposition.
- The greatest fear is that Negroes actually will demand equal status, equal economy, and the right to protect their homes. There are a set of fears experienced by whites as a result of indoctrination in whiteness doctrine:
- Whites fear for their safety, this fear is reinforced by the stereotype and constantly reinforced by the media.
- White fear is not based upon real acts of aggression by blacks but the unconscious expectation of retaliation for hostile acts of whites upon blacks.
- "Fear is the mother of hatred....The lesion that hatred may be expected from those attacked is learned early in life (of whites) and is one of the most enduring attitudes planted in the individual in our society."
- Whites fear black self-defense; the constant assumption of whites of aggressive intent by blacks is very frightening.
- Whites fear the loss of "place"; with loss of place goes loss of advantage, and the sense of security.
- Because of the planter class instituting a black/white society, the greatest fear is and has been since . . . the "fear of equality" in social, political, and economic realms in the American society.

The earliest fears after the creation of whiteness were that of ensuring social inequality, the greatest being those blacks in particular would become the social, political, and economic equals of whites. The greatest fear in 2021 expressed by whites who are attached to the social construction of whiteness is the fear of replacement because of the changing demographics of America—of white domination and control.

CONCLUSION

The inferior black was created to support and protect the mythical delusion of the superior white. White identity has to be reinforced and protected as the antithesis of black identity; white esteem is reinforced by the persistent and perpetual negative images of blacks; psychological defense mechanisms are used to sublimate white guilt and shame. It appears that at every aspect of whiteness, the black is essential, from the structure of the racial hierarchy to the crucial "other" in the four aspects of the promise. Most crucially, the black phobic object is needed to meet core white emotional needs. Who would the white be without the black?

James Baldwin expresses it best: "It is entirely up to the American people whether or not they are going to try to find out in their own hearts why it was necessary to have a nigger in the first place . . . and the future of the country depends on that" (2017).

Chapter 4
Racially-Induced Dissonance

Cognitive dissonance describes the discomfort which occurs when two cognitions (perceptions)—two pieces of knowledge, beliefs, thoughts, or attitudes—are incompatible with each other. Cognitive dissonance occurs when we learn a piece of information, a belief, or an attitude that disagrees with a long-standing piece of information, belief, or attitude that we already have. Racially-induced dissonance occurs when there is a clash between demagoguery of black inferiority and realistic evidence to the contrary, exposing the lie of white superiority and black inferiority.

There are four stages that occur in racially-induced dissonance. The dissonance experienced may result in frustration, anger, shame, social anxiety, or depression. Unfortunately, racially-induced dissonance is so powerful and overwhelming that it is a catalyst for racial violence and terrorism as we will see evidence of in chapters 5, 6, and 7. It is black prosperity and success which incites the greatest racially-induced dissonance and racial terrorism.

There is an opportunity for those experiencing racially-induced dissonance to confront, challenge, and release their former beliefs based upon mythology; most often however, because of the power of the construction of whiteness, individuals retreat into their former beliefs and hold on to them more fiercely.

STAGE I: CONFLICT/CONFUSION

The beliefs about black inferiority—ignorance, laziness, irresponsibility, need for white benevolence, and control—collide with physical evidence that refutes the myth of black inferiority and assumed white superiority.

- Hearing from a white friend that when taking a worker home to the black area, he saw a series of large brick homes. You decide to check it out for yourself.
- "How is it possible that blacks could do this? This can't be."
- Resort to stereotypes: "This is not possible because they are dependent upon whites; essentially children who cannot think for themselves; lazy and irresponsible."
- "They must have stolen the money and materials to do this; these houses must really belong to a white."

STAGE II: COMPARISON

Social comparison research (Suls, 2020) explains how people think about and act within group-based social hierarchies. People compare themselves individually and as members of groups; the focus of the comparison is usually self-esteem and self-enhancement. According to social identity theory (Tajfel & Turner, 1979), people strive for a positive self-view and use social comparison to proclaim the superiority of their own group and its members which filters down to perceptions of self.

Comparison is the second step of dealing with racially-induced dissonance. The white individual compares himself or herself as a member of the white group and then makes a personal comparison.

- How can n—— have all of this, they don't have the intelligence and work habits of white people?
- How can this n—— have what I do not have?

Personal comparison of one's own white state with that of the black confuses what should be a downward comparison based upon mythology of black inferiority; in reality; it has become an upward comparison with a black achievement, with black prosperity, superior to one's own white achievement/prosperity.

- Compares his particular "place" on the racial hierarchy and the "privileges" he receives.
- "They must have stolen the money and materials to do this; these houses must really belong to a white."

STAGE III: EMOTIONAL RESPONSE

Social comparison is a cognitive process that may trigger emotions such as frustration, dissatisfaction, regret, resentment, and envy. Racially-induced envy does not follow the usual pattern, mainly because this comparison is not with someone of the same racial group but rather with the other, the underserving inferior subhuman. The response to racially-induced dissonance is usually emotional and irrational rather than analytical and rational; it is prone to trigger destruction of what the blacks have created.

The white who experiences envy may feel that his status or place on the racial hierarchy is threatened. Racial comparisons trigger strong reactions based upon beliefs reinforced by stereotypes. To retrieve his image as a superior white man, he reverts to the stereotypical images of blacks.

- He feels that even though the black may own brick houses, he is still a subhuman underserving of such and must be put back in his place.

STAGE IV: RESTORATION OF IDENTITY/ESTEEM

Because his sense of individual and group white identity and esteem has been threatened, he must find some way to restore the belief in his superiority. Action may be taken individually or as racial tension builds, collective action may be taken to respond to the dissonance and to restore racially conditioned individual/collective identity and esteem. He will be vigilant about any blacks that he personally finds to be "uppity."

He may choose to insult a black man or force him to demonstrate his inferiority to regain his image as a superior white. Or, the resentment and envy may fester as he waits for the opportunity to act in a collective race-affirming manner to put blacks in their place.

- "I don't know who that n—— thinks he is. I will show him."
- "We whites have to protect ourselves from uppity n——; they are starting to get too big for their britches."
- "We have to show them who is in charge."

THE IMPACT OF RACIALLY CONDITIONED BELIEFS IN RESPONDING TO RACIALLY-INDUCED DISSONANCE

Beliefs based upon the mythology of white superiority and black inferiority are obstacles to addressing the cognitive dissonance which occurs in racially-induced dissonance. Several psychological impairments related to the construct of whiteness interfere with a rational analysis of a condition in which the myths of white superiority and black inferiority are refuted (Bireda, 2021):

- Distorted reality: The individual is unable to see the reality of the condition/situation he is facing; he reverts to a reality based upon stereotypical beliefs; stereotypes are accepted as facts despite what he is actually observing, and what he believes is true is refuted by actual facts.
- Anti-introspection: The individual is unable to engage in critical analysis of the concept of undeserved advantage.

- Inhibition of intellectual growth (Dennis, 1981): Whiteness produces an inability to reflect from a sense of self. "The mental poverty that results from racism must inevitably create minds that are non-reflective, minds that indeed fear reflection. Whiteness decreases the ability of whites attached to the white consciousness to employ critical thinking and analysis. The distorted thinking of whiteness inhibits the ability to judge self and others or to perceive self and others accurately."

There is another crucial value that interferes with the ability of one strongly attached to the consciousness of whiteness to make critical analysis and evaluations when confronted with racially-induced dissonance: individualism. Individualism is a cherished American value which stresses the personal freedom and rights of the individual, self-reliance, and independence. In reality, the promise of whiteness requires conformity to the racial contract.

The racial contract requires that one comply with the professed group beliefs about blacks; it matches the group or racial expectations for whites to consent to and obey the norms of white behavior. In a psychological sense, when one's sense of security and safety, belonging, and identity is reliant upon allegiance to the code of whiteness, one cannot easily enjoy or engage in individualistic thought to analyze the dissonance one is experiencing.

Conformity is the jailer of freedom and the enemy of growth.
—John F. Kennedy

CONCLUSION

Racially-induced dissonance has in the past, especially during the Jim Crow era, led to racial violence against individuals and entire black communities. The tendency and motivation are destruction of what the blacks have created rather than using white envy to create something superior: in Tulsa, rather than destroying the black 400-seat Dreamland Theatre, utilizing the black value of collectivism rather than individualism, they could have gotten together with other whites and built a "superior" 800-seat theater in the white community.

It appears that the refutation of the myth of white superiority and black inferiority is the greatest violation of the promise of whiteness. What fear arises for one who holds tenaciously to the mythologies when confronted with the realization that blacks may in fact be as intelligent, gifted, and talented as whites? And that in the human population, there will be individuals from all groups who possess superior skills and abilities that are not based upon skin color? How can one truly believe in supposed black inferiority and fear his advancement? Where does the incongruence lie?

In the post–civil rights era, racially-induced dissonance is experienced at perhaps even higher levels. The form of violence has evolved to include microaggressions and other forms of political obstruction. Violence remains the response to racially-induced dissonance and a means to restore the white sense of superiority through the use of law enforcement to punish blacks. It is clearly seen in the recent killings of black men and women. The response may also take other forms. A sense of victimhood and despair will be discussed in chapter 8.

Chapter 5

The Violation of the Promise

The promise of whiteness established racial inequality as the natural order in American society in the Jim Crow and pre–civil rights eras. Any thought or perception of equality for blacks was a challenge to the tenets of whiteness and would be resisted and punished through socially sanctioned violence. There were punishable violations for each of the promises:

- Place: Non-submissive attitude, talking back, demanding equal treatment;
- Privilege: Surpassing whites in acquisition of land, material possessions, wealth;
- Power: Attempting to vote, assuming a sense of personal power, uniting for a common purpose/good, boycotting;
- Protection: Owning a weapon, raising a hand to harm a white man, self-defense.

THE NEW SPIRIT OF BLACK PEOPLE

Blacks were engaged in movements for change in both the South and the North. Blacks were leaving the South to find new employment opportunities in the North and to escape the racial terrorism produced by worker shortages in the South. Violent attempts were often made to prevent their departure and to keep them in their place in the South. In the North, competition for employment and housing raised racial tensions.

The return of black veterans provoked fear and rage among whites as their attitudes and demeanor were perceived as a threat to white supremacy. Black veterans took to heart the ideals of making the world safe for democracy and expected the same freedom when they returned home that they had fought so valiantly for in Europe. Black veterans returned with and exhibited less submissive attitudes that the Jim Crow society and white supremacy required. The sight of a black man in uniform represented what was perceived by whites as power and a threat to their place in the hierarchy.

The Ocoee Massacre: November 2, 1920

"Place" at the top of the racial hierarchy was central to the promise of whiteness. The emotional need to remain there was critical. Displacement from this position was a very serious threat that had to be eliminated. In Florida, the threat of racial equality was brutally neutralized.

During 1919 and 1920, in communities throughout the state of Florida, blacks organized campaigns to ensure blacks voted in the 1920 Presidential election for Republican candidate Harding. Black women, having been given the right to vote by the 19th Amendment in 1919, were crucial to the movement. According to Ortiz (2005), lodges, women's clubs, labor unions, churches, and the Colored Knights of Pythias lodge (15,000 of them) all registering to vote was key to the Florida campaign.

Fear and anger seized white minds. Voting was a privilege reserved for those at the top of the racial hierarchy—whites only. Voting would make blacks social equals. Blacks had to be shown that the right to vote or even to conceive of using a white man's privilege was a total violation amounting to a cardinal sin. They must be made to regret even the idea of any political privilege or right preserved for whites. Blacks were warned by KKK members, who paraded through their communities on November 1, that blacks would not be permitted to vote, and if they dared to do so, there would be dire consequences.

On Election Day, November 2, 1920, some blacks did attempt to vote but were turned away by poll workers who suggested their names were absent from voter registration rolls. One prominent black leader of the movement, Mose Norman, sought the counsel of Judge Cheny in Orlando who instructed him to take down the names of blacks denied to vote and the names of poll workers who denied them the right to vote. Judge Chaney promised a lawsuit against the County to contest the violations. Norman returned to the polls with a weapon insisting on the right to vote, a scuffle occurred, and Norman fled.

That evening a mob surrounded the home of Julius "July" Perry, where Norman was thought to have taken refuge. While Perry defended his home, he drove away the mob, killing two of the white men and wounding another. The mob gathered reinforcements from Orlando and the surrounding area. July Perry was found by the mob and lynched.

Blacks in Ocoee committed a number of violations of whiteness for which they had to be punished. They attempted to exercise the right to vote, possessed weapons, raised their hands to harm a white man, and defended their home against intruders. And equally critical was the violation of having more material and economic prosperity than a white man: both Norman and Perry were prosperous landowning blacks.

On November 2, 1920, the bloodiest Election Day in US history, at least fifty blacks in Ocoee were murdered in a racial cleansing and purging of the black population from the area for more than sixty years. Ortiz (2005) describes the defeat of the Florida movement as a historic victory for white supremacy. It secured the promise of white place on the racial hierarchy and racial inequality.

Elaine, Arkansas Massacre

In Elaine, Arkansas, these opposing attitudes—black veterans desiring rights as citizens and the perpetual inequality demanded by white supremacy—conflicted and produced racial violence in the summer of 1919. Vicious attacks were made against black veterans, including lynching of those wearing the US uniform. It became known as the "Red Summer." Elaine, Arkansas was one of more than twenty-five cities in America, including Charleston, South Carolina, Washington, DC, Chicago, Illinois, and Knoxville, Tennessee, that became infamous for the outright—and sanctioned—murdering of their citizens.

The Elaine Massacre of 1919 has been considered one of the bloodiest racial massacres in the history of the United States. Black sharecroppers and tenant farmers, victims of debt peonage, were trapped in a cycle of perpetual debt as they overpaid for rent, supplies, and food, then were forced to sell their crops to owners below market rates. The power of the white farmers was exercised as an unwritten but well-understood dictate by the blacks. No black could leave a farm until his or her debt was paid off. They were exploited at every turn.

Sharecroppers enlisted the help of Ulysses Bratten, a prominent white attorney, to press for a fairer share of the profits of their labor. They believed that joining the Union would help them secure a fair price for their crop and to buy their own land. On the night of September 30, 1919, approximately 100 African American sharecroppers, tenants, and landowners—some of whom were veterans—attended a meeting of the black Progressive Farmers and Household Union of America at a church in Hoop Spur (Phillips County) Arkansas, some three miles north of Elaine.

A shootout occurred between black armed guards of the Union and the three individuals in front of the church. A white security officer for the Missouri Pacific Railroad was killed, the white deputy sheriff of Phillips County wounded by the Union guards and black trustee escaped and reported the incident. By morning, a rumor had spread that the blacks were planning an insurrection to kill whites. Fears arose among the whites where blacks outnumbered whites by a ratio of ten to one.

Five-hundred troops from Camp Pike were requested and sent to Elaine on October 2, 1919, to round up the "heavily armed negroes." They were under orders to shoot to kill any Negro who refused to surrender immediately. Before the arrival of the troops, however, at least 1,000 whites came from all over the state and surrounding states to slaughter blacks. White mobs tortured and killed blacks and looted and set fire to their homes. Evidence gathered suggests that troops from Camp Pike engaged in indiscriminate killing of blacks, often after torture to make blacks confess to crimes.

Within days of the event, 285 blacks were jailed and on October 1, 1919, the Phillips County grand jury charged 122 blacks with crimes related to the event. The charges ranged from murder to nightriding. The first twelve black men to be tried were convicted of murder and sentenced to die in the electric chair. These twelve became known as the Elaine Twelve. Sixty-five others entered plea bargains and received up to twenty-one years for second-degree murder. After appeals, retrials, and a 1923 Supreme Court decision, all of the twelve men on death row were finally freed on January 14, 1925.

Two versions of the events of the night of September 30 exist. The white leaders blamed the blacks for deliberately planning an insurrection against whites, organized by the black union for the purpose of killing white people. The NAACP and Ida B. Wells-Barnett contested the white report as untrue and challenged the allegations and treatment of blacks while detained.

Major violations against the tenets of white supremacy were committed by the blacks in Elaine, so a commitment by the whites to white supremacy had to happen and did. It—white supremacy—was the direct cause of the massacre. Foremost was the assertive act of blacks organizing and joining a union. The dissonance experienced was overwhelming, as blacks who were expected to be submissive and to wait for white approval to take any action operated independently. Expectations from the whites of the behavior of black sharecroppers and tenants was based on mythical beliefs of black inferiority and demonstrated submission. Having weapons and engaging in self-defense was a second grievance; the killing of a white man was unforgivable. Finally, organizing the black union to dispute the word of a white man in reference to how much they should be paid for their cotton was unthinkable. Blacks in Elaine had to suffer massively to avenge these violations.

The psychological defense mechanism of projection was employed very effectively against the black men who forgot their place. Whites precipitated and took the most violent means against blacks; however, it was the blacks, the victims of racial terrorism, who were made to stand trial and be convicted of murder.

CONCLUSION

The new spirit of black people was a direct violation of "place" on the racial hierarchy. Rather than gaining the rights of citizenship from their valiant service during World War I, black veterans returned to racial riots and lynchings. Whites were repulsed by the attitude and demeanor of this "new Negro." The attempts by blacks to enjoy the rights of citizenship in Ocoee and the desire to end economic exploitation in Elaine were both met with violent oppression. Blacks were to maintain an inferior place on the racial hierarchy or get killed.

According to Williams and Williams (1972), "Racism, lynching's, various brutalities, and riots all served as means for the suppression of a new intellectual, economic, and political rise of the black masses that emerged during the World War I period.

Chapter 6
"It Must Not Be Again"

The most grievous violation of the promise of whiteness is black success and prosperity. Black economic prosperity is a direct threat to whites without similar material means because it refutes the myth of black inferiority entirely. The belief that blacks are childlike, irresponsible, and dependent on white benefactors exposes the lie upon which the ideology of white supremacy is built.

The "in your face" success and wealth of Tulsa's Black Wall Street had to be destroyed. The racially induced dissonance created by the realistic evidence of black success compared to the grievous lie of black inferiority was too overwhelming and the individual comparisons of black *wealth* to white unbearable. Rather than face the truth of the lie, whites in Tulsa chose only to see the subhuman black as undeserving: he had to be savagely punished for this violation of white place, privilege, and power. The black intent to protect his family and community has to be viciously punished as well.

GREENWOOD BEFORE THE MASSACRE

The 35-square-block home to 10,000 African Americans was the epicenter of African American business and culture. Greenwood was one of the most affluent black communities in the nation at the time. Their businesses on Greenwood included luxury shops, hotels, restaurants, grocery stores, jewelry shops, clothing stores, photographers, barbershops, beauty salons, pool halls, nightclubs, offices for doctors, dentists, lawyers, a movie theater, and the *Tulsa Star* newspaper.

The self-sufficient community also had its own library, an excellent school system, post office, savings and loan banks, hospital, bus and taxi service. In this prosperous African American community, home to a small elite and sizable middle-class, blacks owned large homes, possessed fine furniture, crystal, china, and linens. Women and men dressed in the finest clothing of the time and drove upscale vehicles.

The Massacre

The usual lie or ruse to engage in the barbarous treatment of a black man or community was the deification of the white woman. In the case of the Tulsa Massacre, on May 30, 1921, Sarah Page, a white elevator operator in the Drexel Building alleged that nineteen-year-old Dick Rowland, a black youth, had attempted to criminally assault her. Sarah Page, when questioned by the police, suggested she would not press charges, and ultimately the indictment was dismissed as Sarah Page did not appear to prosecute the case.

However, the next day, the *Tulsa Tribune* printed the story of the alleged assault and lynching rumors spread. Rowland was taken into custody. Rumors of the threatened lynching reached the black district as well. As a crowd of white men surrounded the jail where Rowland had been taken, twenty-five black men arrived at the scene. They left after being assured that no harm would come to Rowland.

Later, upon hearing that whites were storming the jail, seventy-five armed black men returned. As a white man tried to take a gun away from a black man, chaos ensued; twelve men were dead, two black and ten white. Being greatly outnumbered, the black men retreated to their part of town, what was called by whites "little Africa."

Before dawn, at 5:00 a.m., June 1, 1921, an industrial whistle blew and thousands of armed whites set upon the Greenwood community, looting homes and businesses and setting them afire. Airplanes dropped turpentine bombs on the businesses and neighborhoods. Armed black veterans positioned themselves in strategic locations to defend their community but were outnumbered. By the time the National Guard arrived, most of Greenwood had been destroyed. In her book, *The Nation Must Awake: My Witness to the Tulsa Race Massacre* (1923), Mary Parrish describes some of the terror: "After they had the homes vacated, one bunch of whites would come and loot. Even women with shopping bags would come in, open drawers, take every kind of finery from clothing to silverware and jewelry."

The "comparison" step of the "racially conditioned dissonance" was very apparent during the looting. Men carrying out the furniture, cursing as they did so, were saying, "These d—— Negroes have better things than lots of white people."

As a result of the Massacre, one of the wealthiest and most prominent black communities in America was destroyed. At least 300 blacks lost their lives, hundreds were injured, and 5,000–10,000 blacks were left homeless. The property damage amounted to more than $1.5 million in real estate and $750,000 in personal property.

Why Did Greenwood Have to Be Destroyed?

The Greenwood community violated every promise of whiteness: place, privilege, power, and protection. As threatening to the white sense of place and privilege was black prosperity that exceeded that of many whites. Because of this threat, Tulsa's Black Wall Street had to be destroyed. The dissonance produced by the independence, wealth, and power of blacks in Tulsa had to be eliminated. Various authors have cited reasons:

- "In these years, I have noticed a growing racial hate by the lower whites because of Negro prosperity and independence" (Parrish, 1923).

The "place" of blacks in the American racial hierarchy was still paramount. Blacks were expected to know and demonstrate their place. "Self-assertion" on their part would not be tolerated.

- Rules given to black men taken to the Tulsa Convention Hall for detainment: "Take your hat off, throw up your hands. Be submissive and obey to the letter. Even boys of 10 obeyed" (Parrish, 1923).
- "The causes behind the Tulsa explosion and similar outbreaks in the last few years, editorial observers tell us, are: lynch-law spirit, peonage, race prejudice, economic rivalry between blacks and whites, radical propaganda, unemployment, corrupt politics, and the new Negro spirit of self-assertion" (Walter White, 1921).

The "protection" provided by the promise of whiteness was evident in the Tulsa Massacre.

- ". . . a consensus that blamed the riot on blacks and shifted the responsibility for restoring the Negro district to the victims" (Hirsch, 2002).
- "In fact, the betrayal of Greenwood after the riot was as great a crime as its destruction, because it was carried out not by a faceless white mob but by the men who led the city's most important business, political, and religious institutions" (Hirsch, 2002).
- "Tulsa's bad faith was revealed early on, in its tabulation of the dead. Immediately after the riot, officials issued wildly conflicting figures that kept reducing the numbers" (Hirsch, 2002).

Walter White of the NAACP presented a very different picture of the cause of the riot and its aftermath. "He argued that the conflagration was caused by the white's envy of black success, ineffectual law enforcement, and black radicals demanding equality; he concluded that between 200 and 250 people died, with blacks accounting for 75 to 80 percent of the total" (White, 1921).

Blacks in Tulsa violated all of the promises of whiteness; place, privilege, power, and protection. According to Williams and Williams, 1972:

- "... the black people in overnight prosperity that came to many whites, and some blacks became powerful and wealthy."
- "This fact caused bitter resentment in the ranks of lower-class whites who felt that blacks, members of an 'inferior' race overstepped their boundaries by achieving greater economic prosperity than those members of the 'divinely ordered superior race.'"
- "At least three black persons in Oklahoma held fortunes of $1,000,000 each, and many others amassed fortunes ranging from $25,000 to $50,000.00."

The inequality doctrine was central to the promise of whiteness. The perception of blacks even perceiving to be equals to whites had to be eliminated. Williams and Williams (1972) provide evidence of violations of place leading to the massacre:

- "Another cause advanced by whites stated that blacks of Tulsa affronted the whites with 'radical' action."
- Black people uncompromisingly denounced Jim Crow cars, lynching, and peonage. "In short, they asked that federal constitutional guarantees be given regardless of color."
- The Blacks of Tulsa and other Oklahoma cities dared assert independent agency, refuting the lie of blacks as dependent children who needed white direction and benevolence.
- "Those whites who sought to maintain 'the old white control' could not stomach seeing blacks liberating themselves from the old system."

Greenwood was rebuilt despite the opposition of white political and business leaders and punitive rezoning laws enacted to prevent reconstruction.

As blacks were perceived and believed to be children, dependent on whites, and consequently any black independence was scorned and had to be eliminated. According to Williams and Williams (1972), violence was necessary to entrench the "white imposed fact that black people must remain under the heel of the white benefactor and that they could not survive in this country without the white man's benevolent aid." "The riots were a method to put the upward-bound black back into his place as the Mudsill of American society." Ultimately, white racial terrorism was the method by which the black man was to be kept in his place and to "put down the menace of the quest for equality."

CONCLUSION

Tulsa was a city of two separate societies, one white and one black. The city was deeply segregated; blacks could not even shop in the stores in downtown Tulsa. Railroad tracks separated the white and black areas as they did in many segregated communities. The difference in Tulsa was the mindset of the blacks who established the town and those who migrated there.

Rather than accepting the humiliation of segregation and sense of inferiority as expected by whites, blacks considered their being walled out of white society a blessing in disguise. Blacks were able to spend their dollars in a setting where they would not be humiliated or expected to accept and demonstrate their "inferior" status. They would become "economic equals" by making segregation work for them. They would create an economic center for blacks incubated by the captive black consumers. Greenwood was a world that could not have existed without Jim Crow.

Two black leaders in particular, O. W. Gurley and J. B. Stradford, had a vision for a black utopia. Through principles of collective economics that included start-up loans and pooled resources they created what Booker T. Washington would call a "Negro Wall Street." Indeed, it came to be known as "Black Wall Street."

The affluence of Greenwood attracted attention at a level that local whites resented. They became enraged by the upscale lifestyle—blacks enjoying the same amenities as whites but in a separate and equal setting. They believed according to the mythology of black inferiority that blacks were, despite their economic prosperity, subhumans, undeserving of such luxury.

Greenwood was not just an affluent black community, but more important and more dangerous to the myth of white supremacy; it was a symbol of what was possible for black people in America. Greenwood was an energetic, self-contained, self-reliant, and self-determining black community in which black people asserted their own equality, human worth, dignity, pride, and independence. It was a model for other black communities, where blacks could enjoy economic equality made possible by segregation.

Whites feared this striving for, and demonstration of, that very economic equality that made blacks believe that they could become social equals, and thus that they could, and would, demand equal rights. The demon of "equality" could not be allowed to exist. According to Williams and Williams (1972), as blacks strove to "attain the goals of the great democratic experience," whites saw that their American Dream would collapse, ending white domination. "The frustration of seeing his kingdom come tumbling down piece by piece through economic, political, judicial, and social equality caused the white man to try to mend the cracks by becoming the aggressor in the racial riots of the postwar years."

Chapter 7

The Betrayal of the Promise

The racial violence that occurred in Ocoee, Florida and Elaine, Arkansas was the result primarily of black violations of the tenets of whiteness. In Ocoee, blacks believed they had the right to vote as equal citizens just as whites. In Elaine, blacks sought to end economic exploitation and have equality of economic opportunity. In Tulsa, racial violence was deemed necessary to reinforce white domination when the belief in black inferiority was shown to lack credibility. Each of the above discussed violations against white supremacy rules were carried out by blacks themselves in their segregated communities.

The worst betrayal of whiteness, however, occurred some twenty-one years before in Wilmington, North Carolina, when whites themselves betrayed the racial contract and elevated blacks to equal status in terms of place, privilege, power, and protection. In keeping with the core tenet of the promise of whiteness, "equality" in social, political, and economic life "for whites only," the bloody coup was staged by white supremacists. This act of betrayal signaled the infinite need to prevent any thought of black equality in the future. The overthrow of the local government of Wilmington in 1898 foreshadowed the strict and brutal aspects of the imposition of Jim Crow laws and customs.

The Wilmington Massacre, which occurred on the morning of November 10, 1898, was mob action and insurrection, planned and overseen by white supremacists, particularly the "Secret Nine Society" made up of white political leaders and businessmen. The insurrection was premeditated for months by white supremacists to eliminate black participation in government and to permanently disenfranchise black citizens of North Carolina and return to the promise of inequality for blacks. Virulent racist propaganda by the press that blacks were taking over the city was employed to inflame white attitudes by conveying the white supremacy message to working class and poor whites.

The assault on the black community of Wilmington came from the old playbook of insult to virtuous white womanhood. Alex Manly, black editor-in-chief of the Wilmington *Daily Record*, was alleged to have insulted white womanhood in a reply to a letter by a white socialite Rebecca Ann Felton, supporting the lynching of black men for rape of white women. In his editorial reply, he commented on the historical rape of black women by white men and suggested that some relationships between races were consensual. This editorial published by newspapers across the state of North Carolina stirred a firestorm. This resulted in an ultimatum for Manly to destroy his newspaper and leave town. A mob of 2,000 armed men burned the *Daily Record* to the ground.

The murderous white mob armed with rifles and a gatling gun attacked and killed innocent blacks. The rampage was led by police and US soldiers unleashed to kill law-abiding black citizens. At least sixty black residents were murdered. More than 2,000 black men, women, and children fled Wilmington, stumbling through wintry weather to hide in the swamps and a cemetery. Pleas made by blacks to President William McKinley to send federal troops to stop the violence and protect blacks were ignored.

The coup was accomplished when white supremacists banished twenty black and white political allies. Fusionist leaders from Wilmington, after forcing them from office, replaced them with white coup leaders and escorted them to the train station at gun point. The "protection" element of the promise of whiteness was exercised as no one was prosecuted or punished for the killings and violence. Instead, blacks were characterized as aggressors and blamed for the "riot" as it was termed; thus, legitimizing the coup.

WILMINGTON BEFORE THE INSURRECTION

Wilmington was described as a vibrant mixed-race city, with integrated middle- and upper-class neighborhoods. Wilmington had a busy commercial port and a strong economy. It was the South's most progressive black majority city with a 55 percent black population, a model for building racial solidarity in other cities.

Political Power

Wilmington was governed by the Fusionists (white Republicans, black Republicans, white Populist farmers). The Fusionists was an interracial coalition with a platform of self-governance, free public education, and equal voting rights for black men. The Fusionist enacted reforms that benefited blacks and working-class whites.

- Blacks held public offices as police, treasurer, assistant sheriff, collector of customs, recorder of deeds, and coroner. There were four aldermen, some magistrates, a jailer, and two fire companies.
- Blacks held positions on the boards of audit and finance, as justices of the peace, street superintendent, mail clerks, and mail carriers.

Economic Power

Wilmington had a thriving black middle class made up of professionals, entrepreneurs, artisans, and craftsmen. Black people held significant economic power in Wilmington, and the city was considered by many to be a Black Mecca, a model to show other blacks how they could attain economic, political power, and social status.

- Economic tension existed in Wilmington as many of the craftsmen were black; that is, the bricklayers, plasterers, carpenters, masons, workers in the shipyard, and workers in the factory.
- Blacks worked as mechanics, butchers, plumbers, blacksmiths, stevedores, and wheelwrights.
- As artisans, blacks were jewelers, watchmakers, bootmakers/shoemakers, and tailors.
- As businessmen, blacks owned a majority of the city's restaurants and barbershops.
- Four prominent black lawyers handled a majority of the legal business in Wilmington.
- Affluent blacks in Wilmington possessed pianos, expensive carpets, lace curtains, and hired servants.

The Betrayals of White Supremacy

In each of the aspects of the promise of whiteness—place, privilege, power, and protection—betrayal occurred:

Place: The promise of whiteness was that only whites would be the recipients of high status on the social and political hierarchy. Blacks were not meant to vote, much less hold offices that white men only should hold.

- Edmonds (1951) reported that the great majority of whites in Wilmington resented Negro office-holding of any kind and that the anti-Negro attitudes of the Democrats created an explosive situation in the city.
- Privilege: The promise of whiteness was that economic advantages and prosperity were meant for whites alone. The economic prosperity of blacks and especially their having more than whites was deeply resented.
- Resentment and envy among whites occurred because according to Edmonds (1951), Negroes were given preference in the matter

The Betrayal of the Promise   53

of employment, for most of the town's artisans were Negroes, and numerous white families in the city faced bitter want because their providers could find little work in those trades.
- White supremacy orators asked from the platform, "How many of you white men can afford to have pianos and servants?" Comparisons were made of the black and white man's property, wages, and physical comforts. (Edmonds, 1951)
- The educated and professional ranks of blacks in Wilmington included lawyers, doctors, teachers, clergymen, and businessmen.
- Blacks were accused of stealing white jobs.

Power: Only white men were to control and dominate. No white man could be under the rule of blacks.

- Black men held prominent business and leadership roles in Wilmington, such as architect and financier, real-estate agents, auctioneers, pawnbroker, and collector of customs at the Port of Wilmington.
- Black men held positions as policeman, sheriff, deputy superior court clerk, and black justice of the peace and members of the health board. These positions gave them legal power that no black should ever hold. In these positions, white men were subject to black men; a black man could arrest a white man.
- "The white backlash was prompted not by numbers alone, however, but by the violation of a widely held doctrine of white supremacy. Many whites objected to being summoned before a black judge, to being arrested by black police officers, or to having their home inspected by black sanitation workers. They were unwilling to share any but the most minimal forms of authority with African Americans, especially those who replaced Democrats in political positions" (Chesnutt, 1901).

Protection: Only white men are to have weapons. No black man is to raise his hand to a white.

- As racial tension increased in the city because of the racial supremacy campaign, both blacks and whites armed themselves. White hardware stores in Wilmington, however, refused to sell ammunition to blacks.

The White Declaration of Independence

Aspects of the whites' Declaration of Independence described below are most crucial and telling with respect to the fear and resentment of powerful whites to the promise of the place, privilege, power, and protection of whites as opposed to black; *and particularly the betrayal of the contract of whiteness by other whites.* [Author's emphasis] (Tyson, 2006)

- That we will not tolerate the action of unscrupulous white men in affiliating with the Negroes so that by means of their vote they can dominate the intelligent and thrifty element in the community, thus causing business to stagnate and progress to be out of question.
- That we propose in the future to give to white men a large part of the employment heretofore given to Negroes because we realize that white families cannot thrive here unless there are more opportunities for employment of the different members of families.
- That we white men expect to live in this community peaceably; to have and provide absolute protection for our families, who shall be safe from insult or injury from all persons, whomsoever. We are prepared to treat the Negroes with justice in all matters which do not involve sacrifice of the intelligent and progressive portion of the community. *But we are equally prepared now and immediately to enforce what we know to be our rights.* (*Author's emphasis, added by author to indicate that violence is the usual enforcer and punishment for violations of white supremacy tenets). "We, the undersigned citizens, do hereby declare that we will no longer be ruled, and declare will never again be ruled by men of African origin."

CONCLUSION

The goal of the white supremacy insurrection was to prevent black men from exercising their constitutional right to vote and to hold public office. The insurrection was planned by white politicians and businessmen who used anti-black demagoguery to provoke the emotions of working class and poor whites. Wilmington was the prime target because of the number of black men who served in public office and the thriving black middle class. Blacks in Wilmington had forgotten their "place" in the racial hierarchy. The blacks who returned from hiding after the siege were those suited for menial labor and who knew their place in the now "white supremacist citadel."

Wilmington, 1898 and Washington, January 6, 2021

The Wilmington insurrection was the only coup d'état to ever take place on American soil. While much attention has been given to the Tulsa Massacre of 1921, and rightfully so, the Wilmington Massacre of 1898 was much more insidious. The Wilmington coup was planned and orchestrated by white supremacists as a model for how to eliminate black voters and to restore racial inequality as official policy.

The Wilmington coup is a reminder of when white supremacists overthrew the democratically elected city government of Wilmington, North Carolina in 1898. It is crucial to study this event as there are parallels with the January 6, 2021, siege of the Capitol. While 123 years apart, there are uncomfortable similarities between the Wilmington successful coup and the January 6 coup.

- In both cases, there were attempts to either interfere with or in the case of Wilmington to overthrow a legally elected government. The Wilmington coup unseated and banished elected officials; the January 6 attempt sought to stop the certification of the November

2020 presidential election results and prevent the peaceful transfer of power.
- In both cases, claims were made of injustice, victimhood, that created distrust in the system.
- In both cases, white supremacist militias, members of the military, and law enforcement were key players.
- In both cases, complaints voiced and actions carried out by participants demonstrated an intense expression of anger and rage.
- In both cases, misinformation and white grievances were used to incite participants.
- In both cases, the perpetrators were portrayed as freedom-loving patriots.

The Wilmington Massacre of 1898 returned the once equal Wilmington society to a bastion of white supremacy. We as a nation are in the midst of a racial reckoning, and to understand what we must do, we are compelled to examine the Wilmington Massacre, to ask and answer the following questions:

- Wilmington was a victory for racial prejudice over Democratic principles and the rule of law. What must we learn from Wilmington's history?
- The political goal of the 1898 Wilmington coup was a return to white supremacy. What was the goal of the January 6 attempted coup?
- From Democratic Party Handbook, 1898: "This is a white man's country and white men must control and govern it." Is the fear of white replacement/displacement provoking thoughts of a return to a Jim Crow America, where only whites have social, political, and economic power?
- A major goal of the Wilmington coup was to eliminate the large black vote. Is this the goal of voter suppression laws that are now being legislated across the country?
- "What happened in Wilmington became an affirmation of white supremacy not just in that one city, but in the South and the nation

as a whole, as it affirmed that invoking 'whiteness' eclipsed the legal citizenship, individual rights, and equal protection under the law that black Americans were guaranteed under the Fourteenth Amendment" (Edwards, 2000).

Is the goal in 2021 and beyond to restore inequality as the cornerstone of the whiteness promise?

Chapter 8

The Diminishing Power of Whiteness

Two factors in the last half century have diminished the power of the promise of whiteness: the federal government's changes in laws which on paper at least made blacks and other non-whites equal citizens of the United States; and an economy dominated by globalization in which jobs that were essentially guaranteed to whites were exported abroad.

What would it mean to white people, both materially and psychologically, if the supposedly inferior blacks received equal treatment from the government?

The US government, through a series of Congressional decisions, laws, and signatures by presidents, began the legal journey of creating "equality" for all citizens by refuting the promise of inequality and changing historical US government policy with regard to that concept. It was the landmark 1954 *Brown v. Board of Education* of Topeka, a decision in which the Supreme Court ruled that laws establishing racial segregation in public schools were unconstitutional.

This decision overruled the "separate but equal" principle set forth in *Plessy v. Ferguson.* of 1896. Chief Justice Earl Warren asserted that public education was an essential "right" that deserved "equal protection," stating that separate educational facilities were inherently unequal. This decision faced massive resistance by those who believed that social equality with blacks was a sin of paramount proportion. The

1954 decision became a catalyst for the civil rights movement. Blacks began to defy Jim Crow laws and demand equality for blacks through boycotts, sit-ins, freedom rides, and attempts at voter registration. Violence against civil rights activists was immediate and brutal.

The Civil Rights Act of 1964, another benchmark in civil rights legislation, ended the application of Jim Crow laws which had been upheld by the Supreme Court in 1896. The Civil Rights Act of 1964 signed by President Lyndon Johnson outlawed segregation and discrimination based on race, color, religion, sex, and national origin. The Civil Rights Act of 1964 provided equal access to restaurants, transportation, and other public facilities. It broke down barriers in the workplace as well as provided access to equal educational opportunities.

The Voting Rights Act of 1965 was the most significant aspect of the civil rights movement. The right to vote is an affirmation of one's place in American society as a full-fledged citizen. With this act, the legal barriers at state and local levels that prevented blacks from exercising their right to vote were struck down, and black citizen voting was guaranteed under the 15th Amendment to the Constitution.

The Voting Rights Act prohibits literacy tests, poll taxes, property-ownership requirements, moral character tests, tests on interpreting the Constitution, or, believe it or not, guessing at the correct number of jelly beans in a jar. The act protected blacks from harassment, intimidation, economic reprisals, and physical violence, such as occurred in Ocoee, Florida in 1920, when blacks attempted to register to vote.

The Voting Rights Act of 1965 was the most effective piece of federal civil rights legislation ever enacted. By the end of 1965, a quarter of a million new black voters had registered to vote. This law consequently increased the number of blacks in public office: in 1965 there were only five blacks in the House of Representatives, but by 2021, the number had increased to 57.

The Fair Housing Act of April 11, 1968, a follow-up to the Civil Rights Act of 1964, expanded on previous acts and prohibited discrimination in the sale, rental, and financing of housing based on race, religion, national origin, sex, handicap, and family status. This was the "white man's" government—one that for decades had protected the promise of whiteness—finally yielding to social equality for blacks and non-whites. The government could no longer be trusted to maintain the superiority and dominance of whiteness.

VICTIMHOOD

Bireda (2021) describes whiteness as producing a false sense of reality and validation that can create a sense of victimhood when the delusionary sense of superiority is threatened.

A major reaction to the Civil Rights Act of 1964 was a sense of victimhood displayed by whites. Whites, as in countless times during the preceding 400 years, were seized by fear or even the bigger-than-life fear of special privileges for blacks that would allow blacks to get even. The equality demanded by blacks produced not only inconvenience but discomfort, anxiety, and fear among whites.

The strangle-holding conviction was that equality for blacks should not be achieved at a cost to whites; equality was perceived as a "zero-sum" game. Whites feared they would lose their jobs to blacks, their admittance to colleges, and ultimately that blacks would take over the country. Whites rallied against affirmative action orders and campus policies supplementing the Act.

Rather than a focus on equality and justice to those denied, the rhetoric and position of whites was one of those being denied justice for the *possibility* of social change *to them*. Whites perceived themselves to be victimized by what they perceived as "aggressive" blacks demanding rights that were theirs alone.

The essence of white backlash was a psychological reaction to diminishment of the core promise of whiteness—which had always been the inequality in all aspects of American life for blacks and other non-whites. The coveted "place" of whites at the top of the racial hierarchy was being replaced by federal laws. The "privilege" assumed by whites as their right had always been illegitimately granted because it was based on a delusionary superiority: only whiteness granted access and opportunity. It was now being challenged.

Irrational fears produced by centuries of racist indoctrination had made whites come to believe and perceive that quality and progress for blacks was an attack against whites, that granting full rights to all came at the expense of whites. Whites have been taught to feel there is scarcity in general and that they must fight to defend their portion of the pie rather than work to make the pie larger so that everyone gets a piece. It is a selfish and intrusive teaching, a class denigration manipulating lesser-income people out of upper-class fear. They had no clue that it was the manifestation of Constitutionally stated American ideals.

THE LOSS OF ECONOMIC SAFETY AND SECURITY

If dramatic changes in the social and political climate impacting the promise of whiteness were not bad enough for the whites, economic changes were the final straw. There had been a time after World War II that for whites, the American Dream was truly possible, especially through the provisions of the GI Bill. There were good union jobs, high minimum wages, and a high tax rate of the wealthy that funded American research, infrastructure, and education.

McGhee (2021) terms the economic period in the following decades, starting with civil rights legislation, as the "Inequality Era." Changes in tax, labor, and trade laws altered the economic status of middle- and working-class Americans of all races. The upward mobility promised by the American Dream had become stagnant.

The upward mobility promised by the American dream has become stagnant due to globalization and the deindustrialization of the Rust Belt(the former industrial sector of the upper Midwest.)

- Deindustrialization:
  - wiped out millions of stable American jobs for the white working class,
  - forced income stagnation and loss of good manufacturing jobs,
  - resulted in the children and grandchildren of working-class whites winding up with less job security than their forebearers.
- Globalization:
  - has meant the loss of meaningful employment for low-paying service-sector jobs that offer fewer benefits and take away dignity,
  - global trade deficits have caused stagnating wages, layoffs, and factory closings,
  - the lower middle class has had little gain in income since 1988,
  - the crash of 2007/8 further shattered hopes of a positive economic future.

Rather than being able to critically analyze and accept the new economic reality and exactly where it came from, based upon attachment to whiteness, many lower- and middle-class whites collapsed into a miasma of victimhood and despair.

Studies carried out by Norton and Sommers, cited in McGhee (2021), indicated that whites believed they were now the subjugated race in America, that they were getting left behind, that they were threatened by diminished discrimination against black people, a sign of social equality repugnant to them: "If things are getting better for black people, it must be at the expense of white people."

The capstone position on the racial hierarchy with whites on top fell apart, because, as ever, whites protecting whites from any economic despair experienced by blacks and other non-whites *was not happening*.

Despair

"Power" is the ability to do, act, and produce; to determine the conditions of one's life. Our true personal power comes from within—our inner resources, capabilities, skills, and talents. It is also critically tied to collective efforts (connecting with others, that is, Tulsa's prosperous Greenwood, a community effort).

"Power over" has to do with domination, controlling, oppressing, and exploiting others (Bireda, 2007). The promise of whiteness provided a sense of power over the phobic object—the other, the black. The promise, however intentionally deceptive, met the emotional needs of safety and security.

The promise of whiteness provided the inequality of privilege and the horrible unequal access to employment opportunities denied for blacks for centuries. It turned out, however, that it could not maintain the subterfuge: it could not protect against deindustrialization. The American Dream promised to whites began to slip away some forty years ago, and by the 1980s, "whiteness" on the racial hierarchy was less important than the financial riches of the highest bracket—*the class hierarchy, not the white/black hierarchy*. Jobs that once belonged to "superior" whites in the United States had been given to Third World "inferior" browns and yellows.

Now that the promise has diminished, many whites find themselves in the same precarious economic conditions that had been forced on blacks by the doctrine of inequality. Case and Deaton (2021) suggest that the difficulties blacks faced in the early days of deindustrialization of the cities which led to social instability—substance abuse, unwed mothers, crime, etc.—were precursors of what now befalls the white working class.

Powerlessness can produce feelings of hopelessness, helplessness, insecurity, anxiety, depression, and despair. These feelings of powerlessness manifest themselves in negative behaviors toward others or oneself. In the days of Jim Crow, these feelings were more easily turned outward toward the phobic object, the black. He suffered the aggression and violence caused by any sense of class anxiety or powerlessness among whites.

Today, those feelings are turned inward toward the self of white men, in particular in self-destructive behaviors. Case and Deaton (2021) provide the most revealing research related to the economic realities faced by working-class whites and the impact of those realities, the realities of work in America:

- The economic downturn has led to a steady decline of worker's life expectancy in the United States since the 2000s.
- Mortality of middle-aged white Americans has been increasing since the turn of the Millennium.
- "Deaths of despair," described as deaths that reflect how people feel about their future and value of their lives, killed 158,000 Americans during 2017. "Deaths of despair" have been rising steeply since 2000 among white non-Hispanic Americans between fifty and fifty-four years of age.
- "Deaths of despair" result from three direct causes: suicide, drug overdose, and alcohol-related deaths.
- The increase of "deaths of despair" is confined to workers without upper-level degrees.
- The white working class is driving the upward trend in "deaths of despair." The social dislocation of the American working class is the most crucial background fact.
- Men, particularly young white men in the United States, are less likely to graduate from college, more likely to bear children out of wedlock, and more likely to suffer from "deaths of despair."
- "The deindustrialization of the American rust belt not only drove the disintegration of the working class but also led to the rise of acute psychosocial stress and hopelessness."

Class Status and the Promise

Hewitt (2005) suggests that the most difficult and painful adjustments to the advance of equalities legislation during the 1960s and 1970s was felt by working-class whites as traditional white jobs such as carpentry, plumbing, sheet-metal work were under threat. According to Hewitt, "Although the scale of threat was not known, it was not just the possibility of displaced entitlement that was felt to be at stake, but even more directly, the ability to sustain the family income, feed children, and maintain a roof over their heads that was seen as threatened."

He suggests that the stark economic consequences of change were not experienced as severely by the middle and upper classes.

It is important to consider:

- which class made the promise of whiteness and to which class the promise was initially made,
- which class has the most emotional connection in terms of safety/ security, esteem, and personal power to the promise,
- if the efforts to achieve equality impacted all social classes evenly,
- which class has been the architect of equality policies in the United States.

Ultimately, class issues are deeply woven into race issues; it must be remembered that the nation was initially a class-based society, established by aristocrats, who for the protection of their own wealth and power invented the social construction of whiteness.

When workers are unable to meet their basic needs, provide for their families, and when they lack the knowledge and skills to improve their lives, a sense of powerlessness overcomes them. While the real power of the whiteness promise lies in meeting the emotional needs of whites in relation to identity, belonging, and esteem, whiteness also creates a distorted reality of life in a capitalistic society. The distorted reality of the indoctrination into racial superiority does not honestly interpret the material dangers produced by class status. It leaves the indoctrinated unable to deal with the reality of class status now being imposed by the financial elite, the former "protectors."

A portion Dr. Martin Luther King's speech in Selma in 1965:

> "If it may be said of the slavery era that the white man took the world and gave the Negro Jesus, then it may be said of the Reconstruction era that the southern aristocracy took the world and gave the poor white man

Jim Crow. (Yes, sir) He gave him Jim Crow (Uh huh) And when his wrinkled stomach cried out for the food that his empty pockets could not provide, (Yes, sir) he ate Jim Crow, a psychological bird that told him that no matter how bad off he was, at least he was a white man, better than the black man. (Right, sir) And he ate Jim Crow. (Uh huh) And when his undernourished children cried out for the necessities that his low wages could not provide, he showed them the Jim Crow signs on the buses and in the stores, on the streets and in the public buildings. (Yes, sir) And his children, too, learned to feed upon Jim Crow, (Speak) their last outpost of psychological oblivion. (Yes, sir)"

VIOLATIONS OF POWER

In 2008, the white supremacist promise of black inequality was shattered with the ascension of Barack Obama to the presidency of the United States. The greatest fear held by white supremacists was a "black takeover of America," and the Tea Party was the emotional and political response to this fear of a black presidency. President Obama was elected president again in 2012; his victory was due to the strong support and turnout of minority voters. Obama received 93 percent of black votes in 2012 and only 39 percent of white votes. For the only time in US history, black voter turnout surpassed white voter turnout.

This major violation of the promise of whiteness, of white political power, was not to be ignored. The backlash began and continues: states began to pass voter ID laws and purge millions of voters. In addition, the election of America's first black president ushered in a new wave of white nationalism and an increase in hate groups.

VIOLATIONS OF PROTECTION

The promise of whiteness has since its inception protected whites from conviction or punishment for harm done to blacks. Blacks have been lynched, whole black communities savagely demolished, and black men killed with impunity by policemen.

In 2021, in a very high-profile trial, police officer Derek Chauvin was found guilty and sentenced on three counts: second-degree unintentional murder, third-degree murder, and second-degree manslaughter. This was a rare event in the history of police killings of blacks. Equally rare, three white men were charged and convicted of the murder of black jogger, Ahmaud Arbery. Black protesters and families are demanding more justice rather than the protection historically provided for the killing of blacks.

CONCLUSION

While the promise of whiteness was intended to create a permanent condition of inequality for blacks, the evolving nature of social and financial conditions created inequality for a segment of those designated as white as well.

American culture is one of inequality-based race and class. The most pronounced and destructive effects have been experienced by blacks but came to impact the lives of whites as well, in that the ideology of inequality permeating the culture from the black experience during Jim Crow seeped into the lives of the white working class in the last forty years.

To be the nation that we have the potential to become, equal access to opportunities and treating all Americans—whatever race or class—with inherent human dignity must be our goal. Our future as a nation depends upon it. We are dying on the vine as a country of integrity because of our lack of fairness to all our people.

Chapter 9

A Changing America
Impact on the Promise

The changing national demographics, political power of non-whites, and the economic downturn for working- and middle-class whites have created immense anxiety and fear in those attached to the promise of whiteness. Their fears are related to the very essence of the promise: the distorted reality based on an invented social construct without scientific basis and a myth of white superiority and non-white inferiority.

This myth created a delusionary identity and a sense of power related to the control and domination of the non-white other, especially the black phobic object. Meeting the emotional needs of safety, security, and esteem were crucial to giving power to the promise of whiteness, the promise being to keep the blacks beneath them.

In the past, the fear of blacks becoming social equals and achieving political and economic parity was most troubling to whites. Today, a greater threat seems to loom. Major changes in the future demographics of the United States are even more troubling. "If current trends continue the demographic profile of the United States will change dramatically by the middle of this century," according to a population projection developed by the Pew Research Center (2008). The researcher stated further that by 2050:

- Non-Hispanic whites who made up 67 percent of the population in 2005, will be 47 percent in 2050.
- Hispanics will rise from 14 percent of the population in 2005 to 29 percent in 2050.
- Blacks were 13 percent of the population in 2005 and will be roughly the same proportion in 2050.
- Asians, who were 5 percent of the population in 2005 will be 9 percent in 2050.
- Foreign-born in 2005 were 12 percent, will increase to 19 percent in 2050.

These projections played and rehashed on the news media have created a new set of white fears. The psychological struggle that many whites are facing now is directly tied to their sense of identity. Although this new multiracial America has caused an identity crisis for many whites, they're not responsible for it because the social construct of the white identity:

- bestows on one a natural superiority,
- was created with that promise,
- is a unifying force,
- is the definition of "America,"
- had to be embraced if one was to become a real, authentic American,
- and ultimately is the marker of a personal and national identity.

WHITE FEARS

A major fear is that as a member of the dominant group, the identity that they have taken for granted will be taken away. There are the fears of "replacement" and "displacement" as the dominant identity in America. They will no longer hold the highest "place" on the racial hierarchy.

With the loss of "place" will go the unearned social, political, and economic privileges, power, and unequal protection of the legal system.

- America will not be the same "white" country. America has since its formal inception been viewed as a white nation, one in which the stated ideals are meant for whites only.
- The "privilege" and advantage promised and that has been theirs because of skin color will be taken away. They will no longer have the privilege or advantage of holding a disproportionate share of social, political, and economic resources.
- As a minority, whites will lose political and cultural power. There has always been the fear that the inferior, irresponsible, and childlike blacks would take over; now the fear is of a brown takeover.
- The consequence of becoming a numerical minority is that they will be treated unfairly. There has always been the belief of retribution by blacks, but now the numbers of non-whites (exploited like the blacks) are even more threatening.
- All gains made by blacks and other non-whites will come at the expense of whites.
- Whites will no longer dominate and control America and its non-white residents.

CONCLUSION

Abrajano and Hajnal (2015) describe the hope and fear regarding the arrival of tens of millions of immigrants to US shores. The hope is that immigrants will win over the hearts and minds of native white immigrants and ultimately lead to a nation in which racial divisions are muted and intergroup conflicts rare. The fear is about lost jobs, diminishing wages, increased crime, and the demise of culture, and that will heighten intergroup tensions and lead to widespread white backlash.

Immigration issues are about race. According to Abrajano and Hajnal (2015), "Immigration is changing the United States, but those changes are frequently noticed and filtered through the lens of race." The media has long spoken about the "browning" of America.

- Will the same mechanisms used to deny equality to blacks be utilized to restrict Latino and Asian interests?
- Will a set of stereotypical beliefs be conditioned in the collective white mind about them?
- Will negative coverage of Latinos influence attitudes toward them as has done in blacks?

The distorted reality and displaced entitlement promised by the construction of whiteness cannot withstand the demographic and social changes that are presently taking place in the nation. Social, political, and economic equality must be the core value which determines a positive future for America.

The reality is that America is now and will in the future be a multiracial society with the potential to be a model of human completeness for the world. This is the time that will determine America's internal well-being and moral standing in the global society.

Chapter 10

America at the Crossroads

The potential or actual experience of equality by blacks and other non-whites has historically met with white backlash. The backlash has taken and continues to take many forms, from racial terrorism to protest, to microaggressions. The demon of racial equality and push for such has met resistance throughout American history beginning with Reconstruction, through the civil rights movement and now into what is perceived by some to be our "post-racial" America.

"White backlash," also known as "white rage," is the response to violation of the tenets of the promise of whiteness. Equality for blacks and non-whites, as well as social, political, and economic progress in terms of rights and opportunities for them, incited many whites. Black advancement has historically been followed by a familiar and predictable pattern—backlash or white backlash in the form of violence. White backlash occurs when white dominance is threatened.

There was extreme backlash after the 1954 Brown decision. States refused to implement the "all deliberate speed" dictate. The most intense backlash came from the state of Virginia. Prince Edward County closed its entire public school system rather than integrate its schools. Prince Edward became a model for all-white private schools to avoid integration while no provision was made by the County for educating black children for five years. During this time, African American students had to attend schools in other counties or forego their education altogether.

In addition, the 1956 Southern Manifesto was issued by 82 Representatives and 19 Senators as a form of white backlash. Following the passage of the Civil Rights Act of 1964, racial violence occurred to prevent the equal rights promised by the act. Blacks were accused of pushing too fast. After the Voting Rights Act of 1965 and the Fair Housing Act of 1968, white backlash occurred in the form of gerrymandering and institutional housing discrimination.

The goal of white backlash is to restore the status quo of white place at the summit of the racial hierarchy and to put blacks, in particular, in their "place." From protest and lawsuits with regard to affirmative action in education and employment, to daily microaggressions, white backlash occurs. Until recent years, overt racial hostility was frowned upon by the larger society; Sue, et. al. (2007) suggest that racism has evolved from the older overt public form to more disguised and covert form. Their research identifies three forms of microaggressions: micro assault; micro insult, and micro invalidation.

- "Micro assault is an explicit racial derogation characterized primarily by a verbal or nonverbal attack meant to hurt the intended victim through name-calling, avoidant behavior or purposeful discriminatory actions."
- "Micro insult is characterized by communications that convey rudeness and demean a person's racial heritage or identity."
- "Micro invalidation is characterized by communications that exclude, negate, or nullify the psychological feelings, or experiential reality of a person of color."

These microaggressions serve the same psychological need and purpose of helping the white so inclined to regain a sense of "place" at the summit of the racial hierarchy, racial identity, esteem, and even a sense of personal power.

Bireda(2021) identifies another way in which white place is reclaimed and restored. "Irrational fears related to loss of 'place' lead to the need to affirm one's whiteness through legal and extra-legal means." Bireda states further that "Perverse whiteness is expressed through deliberate and immoral actions designed to cause harm or have negative consequences for the intended victim." The recent rash of "Karen" incidents in which blacks have been out of their place, in, parks, swimming pools, hotel lobbies, and entering an Airbnb are examples. Jogging out of one's place had even more deadly results as in the murder of Ahmaud Arbery an unarmed black man was an example of toxic whiteness, rage, and the extreme obsession with putting a black male in his "physical" place.

RAGE

White rage is the ultimate expression of white power and the norm when white anger and resentment is at its peak. It appears that we have reached a point in American history in which the four promises of whiteness have again been violated in the eyes of the white supremacists, especially in the last two decades as power and protection lost their promised guarantee.

The January 6 insurrection in which a violent mob stormed the United States Capitol to stop members of Congress from certifying the election of Joe Biden as president of the United States is reminiscent of the 1898 coup, which was also the result of the perceived loss of privilege and power. As in 1898, in 2021, there is the belief that whites are being robbed of the promise of whiteness. January 6 was vintage white rage and visible white violence in the face of the advancement of non-whites.

Obama's presidency was a powerful symbol of black advancement and therefore crucial in igniting this sense of the perceived loss of white privilege and power. The anger and resentment were further provoked by black voter turnout and the election of Rev. Raphael Warnock as the first black Democratic Senator from a former Confederate state, which clinched the Democratic control of the House of Representatives and gave Afro-Asian Vice President Kamala Harris the capacity to break ties.

Historically, in the face of the advancement of non-whites, it is the act of ritual violence that reinforces and reassures the promise of inequality. White rage has been and continues to be a reminder of the rules of whiteness and the racial contract. It has been a mechanism for restoring the "place" of whites in the hierarchy. When the slogan "Make America Great Again" is uttered, it is an appeal to return to the time of the promise. It is a not subtle allure to the revival of unequal access to America's resources and opportunities.

The last era in which all four dimensions of the promise of whiteness: place, privilege, power and protection were violated was in Wilmington, 1898. The overwhelming response was absolute rage resulting in the massacre of blacks, all black public officials and their white allies being removed from office at gunpoint and banished from the city as described in the previous chapter. The aftermath of this coup d'état was sustained and persistent backlash against black American progress and equality. It was a prolonged righteousness in support of the lie of white supremacy.

The COVID-19 pandemic and the national and global protests against racial injustice has brought our nation to a time of racial reckoning or racial reaction. We can take the path of those in power some 123 years ago in Wilmington, or we can choose a new path, one in which we acknowledge and correct the mistakes of our past. Which path will we choose?

The social, demographic, and economic changes that have occurred in America during the last sixty years have made fulfillment of the promise of whiteness an impossibility during the present time. There has of course, been the "redemption" of white supremacy after Reconstruction, the results as savage as genocide against Native Americans and the brutal enslavement of Africans. Attempting to redeem the promise of whiteness will have disastrous results for the nation, and America will have absolutely no standing in the world as a pillar of moral integrity.

It is time to turn the page of American history, to start a new chapter; a chapter that is not undergirded by the mythology of white superiority and upholds the ideal of equality for all Americans. How do we begin a new era of American history? There are three paths that must be taken: that of leadership, institutions, and individuals.

- First, we must acknowledge our true history, from its beginning with an accurate description of indentured life, the truth of invention of the social construction of "whiteness" as a means to control the masses (primarily Europeans at the time) and to protect the interests of the ruling class. It is important that the history of America be told with the awareness that the beliefs and actions of each era were based upon the mythology of white superiority and non-white inferiority.
- Second, our national leaders, and institutions, that is, religious, educational, law enforcement, and so on, must publicly and officially refute and renounce the mythology of white superiority and non-white inferiority. It is crucial that leadership promise that no vestiges of the old chapter of American history will remain.
- Third, individuals who are attached to the consciousness of whiteness must seek an authentic sense of identity and esteem not based upon a mythical concept.

Why must the mythology of white superiority be refuted and renounced?

The predominate conversations carried by the media relate to school curriculum and voting rights issues, at the root of both of these conversations is "race." We are still dealing with issues of race almost three hundred years since our founding as a nation because the mythology has remained, been perpetuated, and been reinforced. Espousing color blindness and expressing the most often quoted words of Dr. Martin Luther King, Jr., "I have a dream that my four little children will one day live in a nation where they will not be judged by the color of their skin but the content of their character," mean nothing if the mythology of skin color is not removed from the collective American consciousness.

Laws have created the appearance of equality, but narrative that is the essence of the promise of whiteness remains. The only way to heal the soul of America from the grievous virus invented 400 years ago is to create a new narrative based upon human truth rather than mythology. In the twenty-first century, it is time to release the promise of whiteness that insisted upon inequality for some Americans and to make a new promise; one that provides equal access and opportunity for all Americans.

Developing a strong domestic economy in which as many inputs as possible are sourced domestically is key. When all segments of our population, despite race or class, urban and rural, experience a standard of living that every American deserves, irrational emotional needs, and fears of the "other" will no longer have a place in the American consciousness and we will become the "great society" we desire and are destined to become.

Conclusion

HEALING THE WOUNDS OF MYTHOLOGY

The path out of the mythology of whiteness, white superiority, is not an easy one. Disappointment and sense of betrayal are possible. Fear, anxiety, depression, and even rage are the responses that might prevail. Healing from generations of cultural conditioning requires doing the inner work that leads to lasting freedom from the mythology. The ultimate test of character lies in the quality of "human completion."

If we consider the promise of whiteness to be a stage in the growth of the young nation, and if we are willing to take the next step to become the country that America can be, we must release the unearned status, privilege, power, and protection of the promise and move to a higher level of human development; we must embrace the consciousness of human completeness.

Human completeness is the highest stage of human development; here one experiences empathy, compassion, and the freedom from erroneous beliefs that separate him or her from other human beings. When experiencing human completeness, one perceives unique individualism rather than being bound to a monolith of racial stereotypes; one is able to think critically, to think independently of indoctrination, to open to growth and change.

Conclusion

To know human completeness, one must believe in and practice the equality of all persons and understand human connection versus separation. One can never experience human completeness while embracing inequality. More crucially, as long as one believes in the myths of whiteness which promise inequality, there will always be the anxiety and fear that this illegitimate bestowal will be threatened and taken away.

Cognitive dissonance offers the ability to access the accuracy and function of our beliefs and ideas. Engaging in the following Human Completion exercises will give one the opportunity to confront, challenge, and change beliefs about the "phobic object" that has given one a sense of identity and esteem.

STEPS TO RELEASING THE MYTHICAL SELF

- Self-awareness: What is your connection/attachment to the promise? What needs does the promise meet for you? How can you meet your psychological needs through a non-racial lens?
- Other Awareness: How have you used the phobic object of the black to define who you are? Are you able to see blacks and other non-whites as individuals rather than a monolith?
- Can you release the mythological beliefs about white superiority and black and non-white inferiority? Are you willing to engage in the process of belief system change?
- Are you open to learning more about the beginnings and the impact of the promise on whites as well as non-whites?
- Are you open to building relationships with blacks and other non-whites?
- Are you ready to engage in multiracial alliances to bring equality to all of those black, brown, red, yellow, and white who are marginalized in the society because of race or class?
- Are you prepared to be a conscious agent of change?

CONCLUSION

A true patriot vigorously supports his or her country and is prepared to defend it against that which has not or will not be in its best interest. The mythology of white superiority and non-white inferiority has damaged the moral character of this nation for almost 400 years. As patriots we must release the false sense of humanity based upon mythology and embrace a true humanity. In the year 2022 and beyond, let us make a personal commitment to become conscious agents of change. If a critical mass of Americans become true patriots, then our nation will become the beacon of freedom and equality that it has the potential to become.

Bibliography

Abrajano, Marisa, and Hajnal, Zoltan L., *White Backlash: Immigration, Race, and American Politics*, Princeton, NJ: Princeton University Press, 2015.

Assari, Shervin, *Black Americans May Be More Resilient to Stress Than White Americans*, The Conversation.com, The University of Michigan, September 16, 2016.

Baldwin, James, *I am Not Your Negro*, New York: Vintage, 2017.

Bireda, Martha R., *Pathway to Change: A Guide to Personal Transformation*, Tokyo, Japan: Blue Ocean Press, 2007.

Bireda, Martha R., *A Time for Change: How White Supremacy Ideology Harms All Americans*, Lanham, MD: Rowman & Littlefield, 2021.

Bracher, Mark, *Social Symptoms of Identity Needs: Why We Have Failed to Solve Our Social Problems, and What to Do About It*, London: Karnac Books, Ltd., 2009.

Brown, Danice L., "African American Resiliency: Examining Racial Socialization and Social Support as Protective Factors," *Journal of Black Psychology*, 34, no. 1 (February 1, 2008): 32–48.

Case, Anne, and Deaton, Angus, *Deaths of Despair and the Future of Capitalism*, Princeton, NJ: Princeton University Press, 2021.

Cecelski, David S., and Tyson, Timothy B. (eds.), *Democracy Betrayed: The Wilmington Race Riot of 1898 and Its Legacy*, Chapel Hill, NC: The University of North Carolina Press, 1998.

Chesnutt, Charles W., *The Marrow of Tradition*, Boston and New York: Houghton Mifflin and Company, 1901.

Comer, Ronald J., *Fundamentals of Abnormal Psychology*, Sixth ed., New York: Worth Publishers, 2011.

Cox, Oliver C., "Lynching and the Status Quo," *The Journal of Negro Education*, 14, no. 4 (Autumn, 1945): 576–588.

Cramer, P., "Understanding Defense Mechanisms," *Psychodynamic Psychiatry*, 43, no. 4 (2015): 523–552.

Davis, Allison, Gardner, Burleigh B., and Gardner, Mary R., *Deep South: A Social Anthropological Study of Caste and Class*, Chicago, IL: The University of Chicago Press, 1941.

Dennis, Rutledge M., "Socialization and Racism: The White Experience." In *Impacts of Racism on White Americans,* edited by Benjamin P. Bowser and Raymond G. Hunt, Beverly Hills, CA: Sage Publications, 71–85 1981.

Dollard, John, *Caste and Race in a Southern Town*, Third ed., Garden City, NY: Doubleday Anchor Books, 1957.

DuRocher, Kristina, *Raising Racists: The Socialization of White Children in the Jim Crow South*, Lexington, KY: The University Press of Kentucky, 2011.

Edmonds, Helen C., *The Negro and Fusion Politics in North Carolina, 1894–1905*, Chapel Hill, NC: University of North Carolina Press, 1951.

Edwards, Laura F., "Captives of Wilmington: The Riot and Historical Memories of Political Conflict, 1865–1898." In *Democracy Betrayed: The Wilmington Race Riot of 1898 and Its Legacy*, edited by David S. Cecelski and Timothy B. Tyson, Chapel Hill, NC: The University of North Carolina Press, 113–141, 1998.

Equal Justice Initiative, *Lynching in America: Confronting the Legacy of Racial Terror,* Montgomery, AL, 2015.

Gitlin, Todd, and Hollander, Nancy, *Uptown: Poor Whites in Chicago*, New York: Harper and Row, 1971.

Harvey, Jennifer, *Whiteness and Morality: Pursuing Racial Justice through Reparations and Sovereignty*, New York: Palgrave Macmillan, 2007.

Hewitt, Roger, *White Backlash and the Politics of Multiculturalism*, Cambridge: Cambridge University Press, 2005.

Hirsh, James E., *Riot and Remembrance*, Boston, MA: Houghton Mifflin Company, 2002.

Kovel, Joel, *White Racism: A Psychohistory*, New York: Columbia University Press, 1984.

Ludwig, Gene (ed.), *The Vanishing American Dream: A Frank Look at the Economic Realities Facing Middle-and Lower Income Americans*, New York: Disruption Books, 2020.

Maslow, A.H., "A Theory of Human Motivation," *Psychological Review*, 50 (1943): 370–396.

Maslow, A.H., *Motivation and Personality*, 2nd ed., New York: Harper & Row, 1970.

McCoy, David B., *The 1898 Wilmington, North Carolina Coup D'état*, Massillon, OH: Spare Change Press, 2020.

McGhee, Heather, *The Sum of Us: What Racism Costs Everyone and How We Can Prosper Together*, New York: One World, 2021.

McWhirter, Cameron, *Red Summer: The Summer of 1919 and the Awakening of Black America*, New York: St. Martin's Griffin, 2011.

Menakem, Resmaa, *My Grandmother's Hands: Racialized Trauma and the Pathway to Mending Our Hearts and Bodies*, Las Vegas, NV: Central Recovery Press, 2017.

Mills, C.W., *The Racial Contract*, Ithaca, NY: Cornell University Press, 1997.

Morgan, Helen, *The Work of Whiteness: A Psychoanalytic Perspective*, London: Routledge, 2021.

Ortiz, Paul, *Emancipation Betrayed: The Hidden History of Black Organizing and White Violence in Florida From Reconstruction to the Bloody Election of 1920*, Berkeley, CA: University of California Press, 2005.

Parrish, Mary E. Jones, *The Nation Must Awake: My Witness to the Tulsa Race Massacre of 1921*, San Antonio, TX: Trinity University Press, 1923.

Passel, Jefferey S., and Cohn, D'Vera, *U.S. Population Projection: 3005–2050*, Washington, DC: Pew Research Institute, 2008.

Roediger, David R., *The Wages of Whiteness: Race and the Making of the American Working Class*, New York: Verso, 2007.

Sonnie, Amy, and Tracy, James, *Hillbilly Nationalists, Urban Race Rebels, and Black Power: Interracial Solidarity in 1960s–70s New Left Organizing*, Brooklyn, NY: Melville House, 2021.

Sue, Derald Wing, Capodilupo, Christina, M., Torino, Gina.C., Bucceri, Jennifer M., Holder,. Aisha, Nadel, K.L.,et.al., "Racial Microaggressions in Everyday Life: Implications for Clinical Practice," *American Psychologist*, 62, no. 4 (2007): 271–286.

Suls, Jerry, Collins, Rebecca L., and Wheeler, Ladd (eds.), *Social Comparison, Judgement, and Behavior*, New York: Oxford University Press, 2020.

Tajfel, H., and Turner, J. C., "An Integrative Theory of Intergroup Conflict." In *The Social Psychology of Intergroup Relations*, edited by W. G. Austin and S. Worchel, Pacific Grove, CA: Brooks-Cole, 33–37, 1979.

Tyson, Timothy B., *The Ghosts of 1898*, Raleigh, NC: The News and Observor, November 17, 2006.

Wells-Barnett, Ida, *The Arkansas Race Riot*, Chicago, IL: Aquila, 1920.

Whitaker, Robert, *On the Laps of Gods: The Red Summer of 1919 and the Struggle for Justice That Remade America*, New York: Three Rivers Press, 2008.

White, Walter, *The Eruption of Tulsa*, New York: Nation, June 29, 1921.

Williams, Lee E., and Williams, Lee E. II, *Anatomy of Four Race Riots: Racial Confrontation in Knoxville, Elaine (Arkansas), Tulsa and Chicago, 1919–1921*, Oxford, MS: University Press of Mississippi, 1972.

Zucchino, David, *Wilmington's Lie: The Murderous Coup of 1898 and The Rise of White Supremacy*, New York: Atlantic Monthly Press, 2020.

About the Author

Martha R. Bireda, PhD, is director of the Blanchard House Museum of African American History and Culture, located in Punta Gorda, Florida. For over thirty years, Dr. Bireda has consulted, lectured, written about, and provided assistance to school districts, government agencies, law enforcement, and corporations concerning issues related to race, gender, class, culture, and power. Dr. Bireda has written books related to racial disparity in discipline and personal empowerment as well as historical fiction. Her most recent book is *A Time for Change: How White Supremacy Ideology Harms All Americans*, published in June 2021. Dr. Bireda is a contributor to wsimag.org and is a Florida Humanities Scholar, a historical re-enactor, and public speaker. Most importantly, Dr. Bireda is committed to using her skills to bring about racial healing and racial harmony in our nation.

www.ingramcontent.com/pod-product-compliance
Lightning Source LLC
Chambersburg PA
CBHW032030230426
43671CB00005B/263